TRACING YOUR
EAST ANGLIAN
ANCESTORS

FAMILY HISTORY FROM PEN & SWORD BOOKS

Tracing Your Yorkshire Ancestors
Rachel Bellerby

Tracing Your Royal Marine Ancestors
Richard Brooks and Matthew Little

Tracing Your Army Ancestors
Simon Fowler

A Guide to Military History on the Internet
Simon Fowler

Tracing Your Northern Ancestors
Keith Gregson

Your Irish Ancestors
Ian Maxwell

Tracing Your Air Force Ancestors
Phil Tomaselli

Tracing Your Jewish Ancestors
Rosemary Wenzerul

TRACING YOUR
EAST ANGLIAN
ANCESTORS

Gill Blanchard

Pen & Sword
FAMILY HISTORY

First published in Great Britain in 2009 by
PEN AND SWORD FAMILY HISTORY
an imprint of
Pen & Sword Books Ltd
47 Church Street
Barnsley
South Yorkshire
S70 2AS

ISBN 978 1 84415 989 5

Typeset in 10pt Palatino by Mac Style, Beverley, East Yorkshire
Printed and bound in the UK by CPI

Pen & Sword Books Ltd incorporates the Imprints of Pen & Sword
Aviation, Pen & Sword Maritime, Pen & Sword Military,
Wharncliffe Local History, Pen and Sword Select, Pen and Sword
Military Classics, Leo Cooper, Remember When, Seaforth Publishing
and Frontline Publishing.

For a complete list of Pen & Sword titles please contact
PEN & SWORD BOOKS LIMITED
47 Church Street, Barnsley, South Yorkshire, S70 2AS, England
E-mail: enquiries@pen-and-sword.co.uk
Website: www.pen-and-sword.co.uk

CONTENTS

WHAT THIS BOOK IS ABOUT

This book is a guide for those researching their ancestry in the East Anglian counties of Cambridgeshire, Essex, Norfolk and Suffolk, and forms part of a series of regional guides. The choice of these four counties under the heading 'East Anglia' is because they form a natural historical division which emerged from the ancient kingdom of the same name, and which has been reinforced through politics and geography over the centuries.

Finding out basic facts about our ancestors such as when they were born, married and died is usually fairly straightforward, but this is simply the start. Questions then arise about how they lived, who they worked for, what their work involved or why they moved from one area to another. This is what distinguishes the family historian from the genealogist.

It is a cliché in family history to state that we try to put the flesh on the bones; nevertheless, this is what this book aims to help you to do. There are many excellent books which will tell you how to research your ancestry or provide guides to places to visit. I do not aim to replicate those but to provide an insight into which records can be used to find out what it was like to live and work in these four counties in the past.

The first section provides an introduction to where archives are kept in the region, complementary websites and some guidance on useful resources. As it would be impossible to name every source, or even all of those within certain groups of records, this is a general description of those most useful in taking that extra step to finding out more. Reference will also be made to these throughout the book, along with many examples of the types of information to be found within such records. Also included are places to visit that bring to life our ancestors' experiences.

Beginning the book properly is a general introduction to the history and geography of the region. The next section concentrates on work, trade and commerce, focusing on different themes with a local flavour. Following on from this is a focus on some of the conflicts which have shaped this region. Next are the more personal topics of crime, the poor, migration and education.

A separate section on local government is also included, which describes some of the records generated through the administration of local affairs.

Associated topics are railways and the effect of urbanization on housing. A separate section covers religion, even though this cannot be easily separated from other subjects due to its permeating influence on all manner of everyday life. The Resource Directory at the end includes contact details for the archives, websites and places of interest mentioned throughout.

Unless mentioned otherwise, all the examples referred to throughout this book are taken from documents, indexes, transcripts and catalogues from local archives, family history societies, Access to Archives and GENUKI.

All photographs are from the author's collection and all copies of postcards are courtesy of Mike Bristow *mcbristow@googlemail.com* unless otherwise stated.

Chapter One

EAST ANGLIAN ARCHIVES

Full contact details for local archives can be found in the resource directory. An archive can either be a collection of documents, usually referred to as 'records', or the place (repository) where those records are kept. The terms 'archives' and 'record offices' tend to be used interchangeably. This is partially because most places where records are stored were traditionally known as record offices. A gradual move towards renaming record offices as archive centres reflects the fact that most repositories hold more than just paper records. Nevertheless, within this book I generally use the term 'record offices' as this is what the majority in East Anglia are called.

Most of the archives held in the region belong to administrative organizations that created them for practical purposes that had nothing to do with family history. The largest of these is the Church of England, who had authority over areas of life most people today would not think of as being relevant to a religious organization. This has an effect on where to find records as many were stored with the relevant religious authorities and their jurisdiction doesn't necessarily follow county boundaries.

Boundary changes and the amalgamation of some parishes with others also influences where to find records. As a result you will find some records relating to people from one county are kept in the archives of another. Places on county borders are those most likely to be affected and it is absolutely essential to check which record office has what records. This can be seen with some probate records for Suffolk which are stored at Norfolk Record Office because they came under the Norwich diocese or those for Essex proved in the Bishop of London's court, which are held at the London Metropolitan Archives.

All local record offices have their own websites. Those for Essex and Norfolk include comprehensive online catalogues, but those for Cambridgeshire and

Suffolk are more basic with mainly lists of parish register deposits and summary lists of the types of records they hold included. However, the Access to Archives (A2A) site, referred to under websites, does include a wide range of catalogues from all four counties. Nevertheless, there are still vast numbers of references which can only be found by searching either the card indexes or printed and electronic catalogues within a particular record office. Staff at all the local offices are more than willing to help supply details of resources to those who can't search in person.

All the local record offices except Norfolk include a local studies library. Much local history material can also be found elsewhere.

Finally, whilst this is not a 'how to' book it would be remiss of me not to mention the usefulness of family history societies. All our local societies are active in indexing and transcribing records, much of which can be accessed at record offices and local history libraries.

1.1 Cambridgeshire

Cambridgeshire Archives include the Isle of Ely, the County of Huntingdonshire and the Soke of Peterborough (formerly part of Northamptonshire). As a result, there are three record offices: one for the county of Cambridgeshire, one for Huntingdonshire and the third for the Wisbech area. You will also find much relevant material is held at Cambridge University Library, one the world's great research libraries and home to millions of books, maps and manuscripts.

The Wisbech and Fenland Museum has a dual role as a museum and repository for archives from the northern Fenland area. However, they do make a charge (currently £6 *per* hour) for access to what is quite a poor facility. Copies of some material on film can be found at Cambridge and Norfolk Record Offices, so before visiting Wisbech it is worth checking if you can access what you need elsewhere. For example, film copies of parish registers for Wisbech up to at least the mid-nineteenth century, and other parishes for which Wisbech hold the originals, can be used free of charge at Cambridge Record Office.

1.2 Essex

Essex has one record office based in Chelmsford. It also has access points in Harlow and Saffron Walden libraries where copies of records relating to those areas can be accessed. Most of their holdings are listed on their excellent online catalogue, known as SEAX.

Valence House Museum in Dagenham is the local history museum for the Barking and Dagenham area. It also holds a great deal of general family history resource material, but is closed for refurbishment until May 2010.

1.3 Norfolk

Norfolk has one record office, housed in the archive centre, and a separate heritage centre housed in the millennium library, which is responsible for local history material as part of the library service. Both organizations have copies of much of the material held by each other such as parish registers and census returns.

Two associated websites for Norfolk provide access to a range of references and images from the record office, heritage centre and museums. The first of these is Norfolk Online Access to Heritage (NOAH) at: www.noah.norfolk. gov.uk This includes the entire library catalogue plus references to thousands of museum objects, photographs, newspaper articles and records. The second is Norfolk Sources at: www.norfolksources.norfolk.gov.uk This is a collection of online images of archive material supplied by the record office and heritage centre including broadsides, some wills and administrations, trade directories and some local history publications. Both sites can searched by name and subject.

Some records relating to parishes in the west of the county where it joins Cambridgeshire are kept at the Wisbech and Fenland Museum. This is because historically they came under the jurisdiction of the Bishop of Ely and not the Bishop of Norwich. Just to add one more twist, Cambridge Record Office holds the parish registers and records for the west Norfolk parish of Welney and probate records for the Ely diocese, including those for Emneth in Norfolk.

1.4 Suffolk

Suffolk has three record offices, at Bury St Edmunds, Ipswich and Lowestoft, each covering a particular administrative area of the county. Each has microfiche copies of all parish registers for the whole county (usually up to around 1900). For registers not yet filmed and other records such as wills, poor law records, workhouses etc., you do need to use the relevant office. Bury St Edmunds holds original records for the western part of the county; Ipswich, the eastern parishes and Lowestoft, those in the north-east. An access point is available at Sudbury Library, providing copies of material for the Sudbury area.

1.5 Oral History, Photographic Collections and Sound Archives

All four counties have collections of oral histories, photographs, film and recordings in a variety of formats. Although there are some designated collections and centres for these, there are still a variety of collections spread amongst record offices, libraries, museums and so on.

The Cambridgeshire Record Offices have card indexes in their search rooms to photographs held in their collections. Their online galleries include examples of documents and images from exhibitions on topics such as the Papworth village settlement, sources relating to Nelson, slavery and sport which can be viewed at: www.cambridgeshire.gov.uk/leisure/archives/online

The Cambridgeshire Collection at the Central Library in Cambridge, also has an extensive indexed collection of photographs.

The Cambridgeshire Community Archive Network (CCAN) at: www.ccan. co.uk is a project enabling fifty communities to record their heritage online. Archives include photographs, oral and written reminiscences and video.

The Wisbech and Fenland Museum has a collection of around 10,000 negatives, slides and prints in their photographic collections, which can be viewed there. Amongst the contributors were William Ellis, a missionary who took photographs of Madagascar from the 1850s, Samuel Smith who took the earliest views of Wisbech and Herbert Coates whose work includes views of East Anglia and the east coast.

Essex Sound and Video Archive, based at the record office, is a collection of recordings relating to aspects of local history and culture. Copies can be made at the record office and sound recordings can be listened to at the two satellite access points in Saffron Walden and Harlow.

The Archive Centre in Norfolk, which includes the record office, has a Sound Archive of oral histories. It also houses the East Anglian Film Archive, a moving image archive for the region, operated by the University of East Anglia.

The Norfolk Heritage Centre has a large collection of photographs, a growing number of which are online on the Norfolk Online Access to Heritage (NOAH) website, referred to above.

Other photographic and audio collections can found in local museums such as Gressenhall Farm and Workhouse Museum, and True's Yard in King's Lynn.

Trailers to many of the local history publications, including videos and DVDs produced by Poppyland Publishing, along with extracts from many of their books can be viewed on their site for free. www.poppyland.co.uk

Suffolk Voices is a project to digitize and catalogue over 800 tape-recorded interviews made with local people between 1966 and 2004 and CDs can be borrowed at any Suffolk library. Those currently available include interviews recorded in 1976–1983 of first-hand experiences of the Lowestoft fishing industry and 2001–2004 interviews with Suffolk women about their experiences during the Second World War. Contact Ipswich Record Office for further information.

The Corder collection at Ipswich record office was built up by Miss Joan Kersey Corder from the mid-1950s until a few years before her death in 2005. This includes photographs she took of monumental effigies and hatchments in Suffolk churches between 1957 and 1965.

The north-east Suffolk photographic collection has over 5,000 images of Lowestoft and other parishes in the Waveney District. It includes photographs, engravings, lithographs, postcards and original drawings. This collection was begun by the library service in the 1970s and transferred to Lowestoft Record Office in 1999. Some images can be viewed on the Sense of Place website as detailed next.

A Suffolk collaboration between archives, local studies, museums and archaeology organizations provides over 1,000 images from Suffolk at the East of England Sense of Place Suffolk (EESOP Suffolk) website at: www.senseofplacesuffolk.co.uk/index.html

Woodbridge Library in Suffolk has the Seckford Collection of photographs, cuttings, ephemera and audio recordings on loan from the charitable trust responsible for administering the Grammar School and Almshouses in Woodbridge. It has an emphasis on the immediate locality of Woodbridge, including works by local authors and local church magazines.

The Francis Frith photographic collection online includes images from all four counties at: www.francisfrith.com/search/england

1.6 University Archives

Cambridge, Essex and the University of East Anglia (UEA) all have local history collections. Many are catalogued on A2A, or on www.archiveshub.ac.uk which provides information on archive collections in UK universities and colleges.

1.7 Websites

Details of websites for each record office can be found in the Resource Directory section, and are therefore not individually listed in this guide unless they include specific resources relevant to a topic. Nevertheless, there are some general sites that are invaluable in providing information and access to resources of every kind.

The National Register of Archives contains information on the type and location of archives relating to British History across the country. www.nationalarchives.gov.uk/nra

Access to Archives (A2A) is a database of catalogues contributed by hundreds of record offices, searchable by name, place and topic. Many detailed references to individual records and people can be found. One example is the apprenticeship papers for Alfred Woolnough. The reference to these on A2A from the Ipswich Record Office in Suffolk tells us he was apprenticed at the age of 13 to Samuel Frederick Pells, a cabinet maker in Beccles. www.nationalarchives.gov.uk/a2a

GENUKI is a massive umbrella site with links to resources across the country arranged by county. The individual county pages for Cambridgeshire, Essex, Norfolk and Suffolk also have many links to indexes and transcripts that may not be found elsewhere. Norfolk for example has a set of indexes to local census returns, including some compiled prior to 1841. www.genuki.org.uk

Cyndi's List includes thousands of worldwide family and local links and useful information, including East Anglia. www.cyndislist.com

1.8 Finding out More

Throughout this book there are many references to how different records can provide insights into all aspects of our ancestors' lives. As most records were created for one purpose their usefulness for gathering information about other aspects of life is not always obvious. Below are some those that can assist in gaining a wider understanding of the past.

1.8.1 Apprenticeship and Freemen's Records

Apprenticeship and freemen's records can be found in the archives of all four counties. The largest collections are those for the boroughs and cities and can cover several hundred years.

The freedom of a city or borough granted privileges such as the right to trade and, in some cases, to vote in Parliamentary elections. Records of the admissions to freedom can be extremely useful as one of the criteria for being admitted was to be the legitimate son of a freeman. Others were admitted after serving a term of apprenticeship to a freeman, on payment of a fee, or by being granted honorary freedom. For instance, James Hall of Woolwich was admitted as a freeman in Ipswich by patrimony in 1812. Under the borough's rules this meant he had to be at least 21, born in wedlock and his father a freeman.

Apprenticeship records can be found in city and borough archives, business and private papers and parish records. These frequently give details of parentage, what would be provided by a master in terms of payment, lodgings, food and work conditions and what was expected from the apprentice in return, in terms of behaviour. An example of a parish apprenticeship from Ashill in Norfolk in 1719 is illustrative as it placed a poor child called Mary Garrett as an apprentice to Thomas Rudd until she was 21. It follows a fairly standard format in stating that:

> ... the said Apprentice her said Master faithfully shall serve in all lawful Business, according to her power, wit and ability; and honestly, orderly and obediently, in all things demean and behave herself towards her said Master and all his during the said term ... the said Thomas Rudd the said Apprentice in an Housewifery Manner Influence & bring up And ... find, provide and allow unto the said Apprentice, meat, competent and sufficient Meat, Drink and Apparel, Lodging, Washing, and all other things necessary and fit for an Apprentice ... And at the end of the said term ... deliver unto the said Apprentice double Apparel of all sorts, good and new, (that is to say) a good new Suit for the Holy-days, and another for the Working-days.

A number of indexes, transcripts, calendars and lists exist to freemen and apprenticeship records. For example indexes to the freemen of the Borough of Ipswich from 1320 to 1996 have been compiled by the Suffolk Family History Society, and copies can be found at the record office. Every trade and occupation you might expect to find in a thriving town is listed, from labourer, clerk and mariner to teacher, attorney, clerk and engineer. Although a large number have an address in Ipswich or elsewhere in Suffolk it also features people with addresses as far as London, Yorkshire, Antigua, New South Wales, Malta, Hamburg and Mexico.

1.8.2 Births, Marriages and Deaths

Birth, marriage and death certificates are one of the major building blocks of family history as they provide information on parentage; addresses that can be followed up in census returns; names of witnesses to marriages, informants at death; occupations; ages; causes of death and levels of literacy.

They date from 1 July 1837, when the General Registry Office (GRO) was set up to provide a national registry of all births, deaths and marriages in England and Wales. This is more commonly known as civil registration, as it was a system run by the state, rather than the Church. Before this date there was only a local parish system for recording baptisms, marriages and burials. Whilst it was compulsory to register marriages from the start of civil registration, it was not compulsory to register births and deaths before 1875, unless the registrar requested you to do so. This means that many births and some deaths before that date were not registered.

The introduction of the new civil system was primarily in response to a climate of social and political change during the early nineteenth century. These changes had resulted in the reform of the Parliamentary voting system, overhaul of the poor law system and introduction of census returns to count the population.

There are several commercial organizations offering access to the indexes to births, marriages and deaths online. Those on the Ancestry website can be accessed free in all East Anglian libraries and record offices (and elsewhere). Locally, all Church of Jesus Christ of Latter Day Saints (LDS) family history centres hold copies on microfiche up to at least the 1980s. Cambridge Record Office and the Norfolk Heritage Centre (NHC) both have copies of these indexes on microfiche up to around the year 2000, whilst some local family history societies also have their own copies. Contact details for ordering certificates can be found in the Resource Directory at the end of this book.

If you do not want to order a certificate from the GRO, and know where and when an event occurred you can apply to the local registry office. A full list for registry offices in each county can be obtained from any registry office, in local libraries, online from the Office of National Statistics at: www.gro. gov.uk/gro/content the relevant page on GENUKI and the county council websites for each county.

The FreeBMD website is a free database compiled by volunteers to British Births, Marriages and Deaths from 1837. Although not complete, its coverage up to the early 1900s is very good. www.freebmd.org.uk

Some local registry offices are working with local volunteers to catalogue their local indexes. So far, Cambridgeshire is the only county in this region participating in this scheme, and has an increasing number of their indexes online at: www.cambridgeshire.gov.uk/community/bmd/Camdex

1.8.3 Card Indexes and Catalogues

Card indexes are individual reference cards; usually arranged alphabetically under place names, subject or surnames. A catalogue lists either a specific collection, like those of the Tharp family of Chippenham at Cambridge Record Office, which contains manor court rolls, letters, accounts and papers concerning their Jamaican plantations, or particular types of records such as workhouse or Nonconformist.

Although their context differs considerably from record office to record office these card indexes and catalogues contain countless references to an enormous range of records held in local archives such as manorial records; deeds; maps, business, estate and parish records amongst others. Some references summarize the information contained within a document and include names, whilst others simply cross reference to other lists. Although some of the references from these are included on the A2A website many are not and are therefore always worth checking as well.

One example under the place name card indexes for Sedgeford in Norfolk simply says it is an '1829 census of the poor'. A closer inspection of the document referred to reveals a notebook containing personal comments on local people. Another example is the electronic index at Cambridge Record Office. Searching for the surname Cage brings up a number of references such as a drawing of a tomb; an entry in a manor court book for 1622, a clause from a will and references to entries in parish registers.

1.8.4 Census Indexes and Returns

Census returns are one of the most useful resources in family history as they provide places of birth, help establish relationships and give a snapshot of people, places and households decade by decade. As the UK rapidly moved from being an agricultural society towards industrialization during the early nineteenth century, radical changes occurred socially and politically. These included the reform of the Parliamentary voting system, overhaul of the poor law system and the introduction of civil registration to record births, marriages and deaths nationally. The idea of regularly counting the population via census returns was one of the first responses to these changes, in particular to the rapid growth in population.

This can be seen in the table below which demonstrates the overall levels of population growth for each county between 1801 and 1911.

Year	Cambridgeshire including Huntingdonshire and Soke of Peterborough	Essex	Norfolk	Suffolk
1801	191,751	226,437	273,371	210,431
1811	227,031	252,473	291,947	234,211
1821	270,098	289,424	344,368	270,542
1831	334,391	317,507	390,054	296,317
1841	395,660	344,979	412,664	315,073
1851	455,725	369,318	442,714	337,215
1861	470,174	404,851	434,798	337,070
1871	539,785	466,436	438,656	348,869
1881	622,365	576,434	444,749	356,893
1891	707,978	784,258	468,287	361,790
1901	827,191	1,083,998	476,553	373,353
1911	954,779	1,350,881	499,116	394,060

From 1801 onwards a national census has been taken every ten years in England and Wales, except for 1941 when the UK was at war. Those dating from 1841 are of most use to the family historian as they began to include people's names, ages, occupation, birthplace and relationships within a household. As English, Welsh and Northern Irish census returns are closed for 100 years, this means that only those up to 1901 can be currently used by everyone. The 1911 census will be gradually released from 2009, with sensitive information such as details of disabilities withheld until the full release in 2011. More information on this can be found at www.1911census.co.uk

The National Archives (TNA) holds all census returns for England, Wales, the Isle of Man and Channel Islands. Copies for the whole of the UK can also be used at the Hyde Park Family History Centre run by the LDS church www.hydeparkfhc.org Microfilm copies for individual counties are also widely available locally in record offices, libraries and LDS family history centres, whilst some family history societies may have copies for the use of members.

Over the years there have been numerous projects to index and/or transcribe census returns. Family history societies and LDS church members have undertaken a large number of these, frequently donating copies to their county record offices. The LDS church produced the first national index when they transcribed the 1881 census, firstly on microfiche, then on CD/DVD. The 1881 indexes and transcripts are also available free online on the LDS Family Search site and on Ancestry. Many local family history societies have also produced their own versions for sale in various formats. One good example of a society which has some indexes to census returns online is the Cambridgeshire Family History Society at: www.cfhs.org.uk/Search.html

As with the GRO indexes, several commercial websites host images of the census with accompanying indexes and transcripts. Those hosted by Ancestry can be accessed free at all local libraries and record offices. A large number of indexes in a variety of formats, from printed to CD, can also be found at local family history societies and record offices.

Printed reports to be presented to Parliament have been produced from all censuses which supply a detailed comparative analysis of the rise and falls in local populations as well as changes in industries, farming and trade. All findings were in printed reports until 1966 and copies can be accessed by arrangement at the library of the Office of National Statistics in Newport. Copies can also be found in many local libraries and studies centres. A linked website called Census Area Monitors uses these census reports and other sources to provide historical facts and comparisons about a number of localities over a 200 year period at: www.statistics.gov.uk/census2001/bicentenary/bicent2.html

1.8.5 Coroners' Records

Whilst not immediately an obvious source for general information, coroners' records give us more than just the details of a person's death. Although their survival is variable outside cities and boroughs, surviving records can include details of people's occupations, residences, social conditions and leisure pursuits.

All the local record offices have collections of coroners' inquests, with some such as Norfolk and Suffolk having some name indexes. The Ipswich Record Office for example, has indexes to those for the Liberty of St Etheldreda. One example of how informative these can be is the reference for Florence Maud Banyard in 1894. The indexes give her age as 17, and states that she died of a stomach ulcer in the parish of Melton. The full inquest includes statements from her mother, employer and a doctor which describe how she worked as a domestic servant and had complained of pain in her feet and legs before her death. The statement by her mistress explained how she applied poultices and gave her soda water, brandy and water as a treatment, whilst Dr Elphinstone Hollis was 'of the opinion the deceased died from an ulcer in the stomach which had probably existed for some years [and] perforated the stomach giving rise to peritonitis'.

1.8.6 Maps

All local archive centres have a good selection of maps, including estate, tithe and enclosure. Many of these will be referred to throughout this book, so what follows is a brief introduction to those that are of most helpful to the family historian.

Maps illustrate the physical changes on the landscape of events such as enclosure and industrialization. This is illustrated by the first large-scale map of Norfolk which was published in 1797 by William Faden, Geographer to the King. Within fifteen years of publication the extensive commons, heaths and warrens had largely disappeared. Original copies of the map are rare, as is the copy produced by the Norfolk Record Society in 1975. More easily available are the edition produced by Larks Press in 1989 with an introduction by J C Barringer, and the digital redrawing undertaken by Andrew Macnair which can be explored at: www.fadensmapofnorfolk.co.uk

Enclosure maps and their accompanying awards include details of commons and open fields, many of which had disappeared by the time the tithe maps were compiled around 1840. They specify the public or private status of roads and paths and who had responsibility for maintaining hedges and the names of landowners. They also include details of charity land, the income from which would be distributed amongst the poor.

The process of enclosing open fields or common land by putting a hedge or fence around it has been going on for hundreds of years and could be done by agreement between landowners. Parliamentary enclosure meant this process was formalized. The majority of enclosure maps, also known as 'inclosure', date from after the first General Enclosure Act was passed in 1801 and can be found in local record offices. However, it is also possible to find maps associated with earlier private acts along with other records which

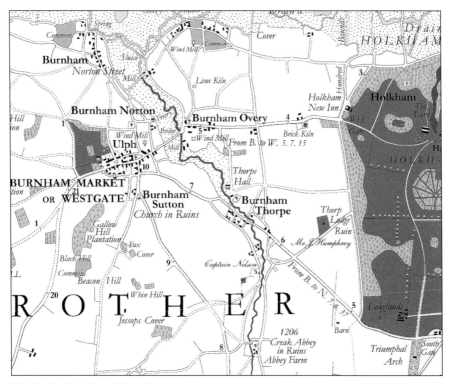

Digitized redrawing of Faden's 1797 map showing Burnham Thorpe in Norfolk. (courtesy of Andrew Mcnair)

detail ownership, tenancies, and the use and value of the land to which they refer.

Tithes were originally payments of farm produce in kind (crops, wool, milk etc.) made by parishioners to support the parish church and clergy. This was replaced by a money payment in 1836 under the Tithe Commutation Act. Each map shows at least the boundaries of woods, fields, roads and waterways as well as the location of buildings. Their accompanying apportionment lists the owners and occupiers, the acreage of land occupied, type of cultivation and its tithe valuation. Three copies were made, one for the tithe commissioners, one for the Diocese and one for the parish, so many copies can be found locally.

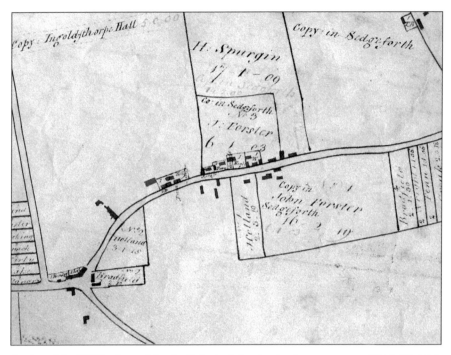

Section of the 1797 Inclosure Map for Sedgeford showing landowners names. (NRO: PD 601 / 150)

As the tithe maps were mainly produced between 1836 and 1842, many people listed on the 1841 census will be included, enabling you to locate them within their physical environment. Again, there are also a range of publications featuring maps both in print and online. One of these is *Suffolk Snapshots* by Suzanna G Burnay (Sigma Books). This is a series of booklets providing a snapshot of some Suffolk villages in the 1840s using information taken from maps, the 1841 census and parish records. The same author is also developing a series of indexes to people listed in the tithe apportionments.

Ordnance Surveys were the first accurate maps of the country. The Ordnance Survey was founded in 1791 at the height of the French Revolution, amidst concerns of French invasion. Within twenty years around a third of England and Wales had been mapped at the one-inch to the mile scale. From the 1830s surveys of England and Wales at the six-inch to the mile scale were produced and the Ordnance Survey Act of 1841 meant all public boundaries had to be surveyed, although some counties were not surveyed until much later. Copies of surviving maps can be found in both The National Archives and local archives, with some available online.

Many local archives also hold copies of the Aerial Survey conducted by the Royal Air Force in 1945–6 to help with the revision of maps as well as highways and planning work. This provides a record of the landscape at that time and is used today in conjunction with later surveys for research into land use, planning, coastal erosion, local history and so on.

Other maps that record information about people and places dating back several centuries include estate maps, town and county maps, and road, railway and canal plans from 1792. Maps can also be found amongst other collections of records such as sales particulars, business papers and manorial records.

Many images of maps can be found online, and the best source for finding these is the individual county pages on GENUKI. One extremely useful initiative is the Norfolk E Map Explorer website which allows a search to be made of copies of the first Ordnance Survey Map, the 1946 Aerial Survey, some Enclosure and the Tithe Maps for Norfolk. The various maps can be compared side by side and even overlaid to show changes. www.historic-maps.norfolk.gov.uk/Emap/EMapExplorer.asp?PID=0

1.8.7 Newspapers

Newspapers provide information on every aspect of our ancestors' lives. For example, when Ilford man William Knightley died in an accident in Shoreditch in 1909, his death and inquest were reported in both the *County and City of London Observer* and the *Ilford Guardian*, followed by an obituary and funeral report which mentioned his occupation, address, relatives and involvement in local affairs and good causes.

Looking at local and national newspapers for key dates in our ancestors' lives is an extremely good way to find out more about what was going on locally and nationally that would have affected them. For instance, if your ancestor was born married or died in Norwich in October 1819 you would find reports in local papers about the provision of playing fields and open spaces in Norwich. These were indicative of a wider trend in the nineteenth century which aimed to improve the health and wellbeing of people through public works such as drainage schemes, lighting, play areas, parks and public baths, where people could wash and do their laundry, and were widely reported

Newspapers are also an excellent resource for finding out more about people's leisure activities and sporting endeavours. For example, reports in the *Norfolk Chronicle* in March 1822 described how Wombwell exhibited his menagerie on the Castle Meadow in Norwich, and the impersonator Mr Blanchard had appeared at Norwich Theatre. In contrast, the *Norfolk Chronicle* in 1872 reported that local peer Lord Walsingham killed 842 head of grouse between 5.30 a.m. and 3 p.m. while shooting on Blubberhouse Moor in Yorkshire.

Transcripts from the *Beccles and Bungay Weekly News* (available on the GENUKI Suffolk site) provide insights into many other aspects of life. In the case of a report about a bazaar held in July 1862 to raise money to reduce the debt on the Bungay Wesleyan Chapel, it shows that fundraising activities are nothing new. It describes the many attractions and names the organizers, as well as giving a special mention to 'Mr Boatwright with his photographic cameras'.

The national newspaper library at Colindale in north London has collections of local and national newspapers from all over the UK. There are also comprehensive collections of local papers in the East Anglian record offices and local studies libraries.

Indexes to all pictures from Cambridgeshire newspapers from 1916–34, and a cuttings file from 1954 can be found in the Cambridgeshire Collection held at the Central Library. A link to extracts from the *Soham Chronicle*, 1787–1899 can be found on the GENUKI Cambridgeshire page. *Cambridgeshire and Opinion, 1780–1850* by Michael Murphy (Cambridge, 1977) examines the interaction between local press and public opinion, including many extracts.

Essex Record Office has copies of several local newspapers, with the earliest dating from 1720, although most were published from the early to mid-nineteenth century onwards. They have produced a book called *Headline History* (2000) featuring articles taken from the *Essex Chronicle* over a hundred years, with an accompanying summary of the historical events referred to and a CD of recorded interviews from the Essex Sound Archive.

Norfolk has the *Norfolk Annals*, extracts taken from *The Norfolk Chronicle* between 1800 and 1900, at both the record office and heritage centre. The heritage centre has a collection of selective news-cuttings of obituaries and general interest articles dating from the early 1900s to the 1980s. Some extracts from the *Norfolk Chronicle* also appear on the GENUKI Norfolk page. The NOAH website has online indexes to local newspapers from 1922 to 1978.

In Suffolk, there is growing collection of card indexes at each office, focusing on the main newspaper for their area up to around the mid 1800s. There are also boxes of news-cuttings arranged alphabetically by name, place and subject in the search room which go well into the twentieth century.

Transcripts for some years of the *Beccles and Bungay Weekly News* can also be found the GENUKI Suffolk page. Taking some entries from the year 1862 as an example, there is a prosecution of William Barber, William Baker and Henry Pitts for playing pitch-halfpenny on Bungay Common on a Sunday, an advertisement from Bungay fishmonger, John Tillett, and the death in Beccles of Susan, daughter of Robert Took, a postman.

The Foxearth District Local History Society is dedicated to publishing research materials relating to the area around the parishes of Borley, Foxearth, Liston and Pentlow in Essex and Suffolk. Amongst those on their website are a large number of transcriptions from local newspapers from 1740 to the 1950s. www.foxearth.org.uk/index.html

Many local libraries and archive centres have a licence agreement allowing access to *The Times* from 1785 to 1985 which can be searched using key words.

1.8.8 Parish Records

Parish registers of baptisms, marriages and burials are the most well known and commonly used parish records. There is however, a diverse range of other records relating to the administration of parish affairs, originally kept in the parish chest, which can add insights and essential information about the people who lived, worked or passed through each parish. This is because the parish formed the basis of local government until the nineteenth century. The law was enforced by the parish constable; the poor were cared for by the overseers elected by the ratepayers; highways were maintained under supervision of a surveyor elected by the villagers; commons and open fields would be managed by either an elected officer, or by the parish itself through a the vestry meeting (a kind of petty Parliament). Most surviving parish records, including parish registers, have been deposited in record offices.

Again, many of the records generated by these activities will be featured throughout this book, but the main categories include poor law records, churchwardens' accounts, detailing taxes and payments towards maintaining the fabric of the church and relieving the poor, charity records, collections for good causes (briefs), plans, school records, wills of benefactors, and terriers recording church possessions such as lands, houses, stock and tithes.

Other records to be found range from lists of 'strange preachers', notices and proclamations, faculties and licences. One very useful series of records is the vestry minute book which records disputes over the rating of buildings or land, the administration of common property, the making of by-laws, and levies and expenditure relating to the poor, such as the provision of clothing and apprenticing of pauper children, as well as lists of emigrants and any parish funds provided towards their passage.

1.8.9 Probate Records

Wills, administrations and inventories are one of the best genealogical records available to us. Not only do they name relatives, but they may describe the property and personal goods your ancestors owned, reveal their favourite charities, explain family feuds and expose scandals. They are also some of the few documents written in ordinary people's own words, shedding light on their attitudes, lifestyles and the social and political conditions of the time. For example, when Margaret Cage of Burrough Green in Cambridgeshire left a will in 1624 she bequeathed watches, gold rings and money to her brothers, her sister, sister-in-law, brother-in-law, nieces and nephews and a cousin. In contrast, when James Mann of Hackford in Norfolk left a will in 1886 he named his illegitimate son, John, by his housekeeper, Alice Howlett.

Probate records can also include details of property ownership, household goods and social status. For instance, when Robert Futter of South Burlingham left a will in 1821, he described his tenements, cordwainer shop, and garden, land and allotment, in various parishes, and who the occupiers were.

Before 1858, probate records were generally administered by church courts and the majority of these are held locally. As a result, there was no single system or place in which wills were proved before this date.

Locating probate records before 1858 can be complicated. In Cambridgeshire, the Cambridge Record Office has either the originals or microfilm copies of probate records for the Courts of the Consistory of Ely (including Emneth in Norfolk), the Archdeaconry of Ely, the Peculiar of Thorney and Vice-Chancellor of Cambridge University.

Huntingdon Record Office has probate records for the Courts of the Archdeaconry of Huntingdon and the Peculiar's of Stow Longa, Spaldwick, Brampton and Buckden. Probate records for a small number of Cambridgeshire parishes can also be found in the Norwich Consistory Court and are kept at the Norfolk Record Office.

The majority of probate records for Essex people before 1858 are held at the Essex Record Office. However, some were proved in the Consistory Court of the Bishop of London and are kept at the London Metropolitan Archives. Others were proved in the Commissary Court of the Bishop of London and the Peculiar of the Dean and Chapter of St Paul's and are kept at the Guildhall Library in London.

Suffolk is divided between the Archdeaconry of Suffolk and the Archdeaconry of Sudbury. The Archdeaconry of Suffolk covers the east of the county and these probate records are held at the Ipswich Record Office. The Archdeaconry of Sudbury covers the west of the County and these are held at Bury St Edmunds Records Office.

The Record Office at Bury St Edmunds also holds probate records for the Deanery of Fordham, which includes some Cambridgeshire parishes, as well as those for the parish of Freckenham, which was part of the Peculiar of Isleham and Freckenham. The Suffolk parishes of Monks Eleigh, Moulton and Hadleigh are part of the Deanery of Bocking, Essex, and are held at Essex Record Office.

Norfolk had three main church courts which dealt with probate records: The Archdeaconry of Norfolk was responsible for around 400 parishes and the Archdeaconry of Norwich for around 300. The Norwich Consistory Court had overriding jurisdiction over most of the county as well as most of Suffolk and a few Cambridgeshire parishes. There are also the Peculiar Courts of the Dean and Chapter, Great Cressingham and Castle Rising and Borough Courts for Norwich, King's Lynn and Yarmouth. All these records can be accessed at the Norfolk Record Office and Norfolk Heritage Centre.

Indexes to wills and administrations for all four counties can be found in all local record offices in a variety of formats from the original indexes to card, printed and electronic indexes. Other organizations such as family history societies also have copies of some or all indexes. Many record offices are adding their probate indexes to their online catalogues, with some such as Norfolk, including digitized images (see Norfolk Sources website).

The Prerogative Court of Canterbury (PCC) had jurisdiction over the whole of England and Wales, so includes many wills and administrations of people from East Anglia. These can be accessed at The National Archives. The PCC wills are indexed on The National Archives Documents Online website with the option to buy digitized copies. Some printed indexes to the PCC wills and administrations for various years, can be found in local record offices.

After 1858 a national system came into force. Whilst probate records after this date are held at the Principal Probate Registry, copies of wills and administrations, granted locally between 1858 and the 1940s locally, can be found in some local archives. It is also possible to find indexes to probate records from 1858 locally. The Norfolk Heritage Centre has copies for the whole of England and Wales up to 1966, whilst Essex Record Office has the same indexes up to 1943. The Suffolk record offices on the other hand have various indexes just relating to Suffolk people up to the 1920s.

1.8.10 *Property Records*

A diverse range of property records exist amongst collections of private and estate papers, business records and manorial records. These include deeds, leases, sales particulars, maps, accounts and tenancy records. All these can supply a wealth of detail about people and events within a neighbourhood.

Manorial Courts registered any transactions relating to land copyhold of a manor whether by inheritance, sale, lease etc. up to 1922 when the system was abolished. Every time one of these transfers took place the court books would note how the person holding that land or property, had come to hold it in the first place. This means that if someone inherited property the court books would refer to that. The Vincent family from the Whinburgh and Westfield area of Norfolk are a good example, as the Westfield manorial records have assisted in establishing their family relationships back to the late 1500s.

There are many other sources associated with property ownership or tenancy that list individuals and households. These include voting registers and hearth, land and window tax records, dating from the seventeenth to nineteenth centuries. Amongst the various indexes and transcripts that exist are those to Essex poll books, hearth tax returns and land tax assessments and the 1780 Cambridgeshire tax on male servants. Although such records do not include everyone or provide birthplaces, they show where people were living and give an idea of their status in a community.

Quarter Sessions and Petty Sessions court records include many references to where people lived, especially when there were disputes over boundaries, highways maintenance or rights of way. The Essex Quarter Sessions papers for 1843 for example include a report from the constabulary committee regarding a complaint from a Mrs Griggs referring to the state of the fences between her property and the station at Springfield.

1.8.11 Publications

Numerous local histories, biographies, genealogies, indexes and transcripts have been produced over the years. In some cases the sources used at that time may no longer survive or be in much poorer condition. Others may be translations of Latin documents making these accessible to a wider audience. Reference copies can generally be found in local record offices and local studies libraries. An example is *The Frogley Index and Manuscript*. It contains potted histories of people and places in the Barking area of Essex, compiled by Mr Frogley, and was donated to the Essex Archaeological Society in 1939. The original is now kept at Valence House Museum and the East London Family History Society has produced a digitized copy on CD.

Record Societies were founded for the purpose of publishing editions of original documents and unavailable printed works and historical maps for each county in order to make them more accessible (see Resource Directory for contact details). Those published by the Cambridgeshire Records Society, for example, include documents relating to the history of the King's School in Ely, over six centuries; the accounts of the rector of Fowlmere from 1682 to 1710, which details local corn prices, marketing, yields, the operation of open fields and farming practices; the nineteenth century diaries of Joseph Romilly, a Fellow of Trinity College and Registrar of the University of Cambridge, and various manorial records for the county.

Suffolk Records Society publications include the archives of the Abbey of Bury St Edmunds; the journal of Frenchman Francois de la Rochefoucauld, reflecting on the year he spent based in Bury St Edmunds in 1784; various manorial court rolls; will abstracts and the casebook for the period 1839 to 1841 of a junior hospital doctor based at Suffolk General Hospital.

The *Consistory Court Depositions, 1499–1512; 1518–1530* published by the Norfolk Record Society gives an idea of the range of topics and information that can be gleaned through such publications. The 1520 deposition regarding the will of Thomas Craske of Sudbury in Suffolk is a good example. As well as referring to property and bequests to family members, it includes the following statement that raises all kinds of questions and inferences about the personal relationship of the couple referred to:

John Powley (3), of Sudbury, res. 20 years, deposed that the testator made his will 2 years before. His brother Dns. Robert Craske was present and asked him, 'What will you give your wif?' and he replied 'I will hir nothing, because she never lovyd me'. After a while Dns. Robert Craske asked him 'Will it please you to gif her yor monea bills? and he answered, 'I am content as ye will'.

1.8.12 Trade Directories and Gazetteers

These provide a geographical guide, short histories, descriptions of places and listings of those in trade throughout the nineteenth and early twentieth centuries, and occasionally earlier. Even if your ancestor is not listed you will get a 'feel' for the environment in which they lived, who they might have worked for, the main types of work available in that area, where they went to school etc.

For instance, Marks Tey in Essex in the late 1870s had a brick, tile and pipe manufacturer, a carpenter and wheelwright, shopkeeper, maltster, blacksmith, grocer and corn and seed merchant. It also had a post office, three pubs, a national school built in 1866 for 120 children and a railway station.

The Historical Directories website hosts a national collection for some decades. www.historicaldirectories.org/hd Many have also been published on CD by commercial organizations. It is also possible to find many local directories at record offices, heritage centres and family history societies. A number of indexes and transcripts also appear on the relevant county pages on GENUKI. For instance, John Walesby senior, a saddler in Bungay, is listed on an alphabetical index to Pigot's 1823–24 trade directory on the Suffolk page.

1.8.13 Writers and Diarists

East Anglia has a rich collection of contemporary writings in letters, diaries and fiction. Whilst these voices are undoubtedly affected by the writers' social class, race or gender, they still give us a 'voice' from particular periods of time. Many have been published, but all archives have unpublished collections which can only be accessed there.

Amongst the best known are the medieval letters of the Paston family from Norfolk, which have been published extensively over the years. Others to recommend include the published diaries of Parson James Woodforde, vicar of the small village of Weston Longville from 1774 until his death in 1803. His daily diaries record the minutiae of day to day life, local news and national events.

In Suffolk, Richard Cobbold's 1860 account of Wortham is a moving record of village life as seen by the local rector. Another local clergyman who kept a diary was John Longe, vicar of Coddenham in the late eighteenth and early nineteenth centuries. Both of these have been published.

George Ewart Evans (1909–1988) was a pioneer in collecting oral histories. Before moving to Brooke in Norfolk in 1968, he lived in Suffolk for many years where he collected reminiscences about Suffolk rural customs and way of life. His books include *Ask the Fellows who Cut the Hay* (1956), *Where Beards Wag All* (1970), *The Days That We Have Seen* (1975) and *The Strength of The Hills* (1983).

We can also add the fiction writers of their time who took their inspiration from the landscape, people and events around them. One such was the Norfolk novelist Mary Mann who produced thirty-nine books before her death in 1929, portraying the class system and poverty of Norfolk in the late nineteenth and early twentieth centuries. Her first book, *The Parish of Hilby* was based on the village of Shropham where she lived.

Another instance is the book *Akenfield: Portrait of an English Village* by historian Ronald Blythe, which portrays the economic and social life of a village in East Anglia. *Akenfield* is a made-up place name based partly upon Akenham, a small village just north of Ipswich, and probably on Charsfield near Wickham Market. It was made into a successful film in 1974 which was filmed on location in villages nearby, with Blythe playing the vicar and local villagers playing all the other parts.

Chapter Two

INTRODUCTION TO THE REGION

East Anglia is an extremely diverse region with a common denominator of big sky and lots of water. Although it is frequently described as flat (most famously by Noel Coward when referring to Norfolk), this is not strictly true. Whilst generally a lowland, it dips and flows, allowing its big sky to dominate. The four counties have many physical features in common, especially in adjoining areas, as well as mutual social, historical and political experiences. They do nevertheless have their own individual characteristics and quirks.

The coast and waterways form an essential part of the region's geography and every aspect of its history as the places where people lived, worked and played. Changes to the coastline have been well documented over many centuries. As early as the late 1300s extreme weather patterns contributed to the harbour at Great Yarmouth becoming silted up, whilst tidal changes on the Lincolnshire coast shifted millions of tons of sand and shingle onto the north Norfolk coast. In Burnham Thorpe, for instance, it was recorded in 1400 that the 'sea had gone back and river become embanked'. Five hundred years later, the local rector described how the mouth of the Burn had been forced nearly a quarter of a mile eastwards between 1920 and 1936.

Serious erosion can be seen at Covehithe in Suffolk, where the road comes to an abrupt end, whilst Dunwich, once the seat of Saxon kings and an affluent port, has been gradually destroyed. Within living memory, the 1953 east coast floods caused devastating damage when a combination of gale force north-westerly winds and exceptionally high tides created a tidal surge that smashed through coastal defences. Over 300 people died and 24,000 houses were flooded.

The three counties of Norfolk, Suffolk and Essex are very similar physically, being almost completely separated from the rest of England. The southern

Bishops Bridge Road in Norwich during the 1912 floods.

half of Cambridgeshire close to Cambridge is very similar to nearby Essex with its rolling chalk hills. In contrast, the northern half, including the Isle of Ely and part of the Great Bedford Level, is a large flat expanse formed out of the drained Fens.

East Anglia's history and character has been formed over the centuries by a mix of wars and threat of invasion from the east, while the native population has assimilated with Roman, Saxon, north-east French, Low Country, German and Scandinavia settlers and invaders. Numerous new towns, ports and roads were built under the Romans, with the remains of many of those roads still surviving as green tracks, hedges and parish boundaries.

One of the most important was the thirty-five mile route across west Norfolk, now known as the Peddars Way footpath, which was probably military in origin and may have served as an approach to a Roman Ferry across the Wash. The Fen Causeway provided access through the Fens from the north and west of England to East Anglia and was still used within living memory by cattle drovers from Scotland and the north, bringing cattle to north Norfolk.

Another vital road is the Roman road known as 'Stanestreet' between Colchester and St Albans. This was so well used that in 1530 the canons of Thremhall Priory, just north-west of the road, complained about the number of travellers going to them for hospitality. In the seventeenth century the Great Newmarket road (formerly the A11 and now the B1383) was improved so Charles II could travel quickly between his palaces and mistresses in London and his stables in Newmarket. This became one of the busiest roads in the country, with the eighteenth century diarist, Parson Woodforde, describing it as one of the best he had ever travelled.

As the Roman Empire began to disintegrate, Anglo-Saxon settlers from the German regions of Angeln and Saxony made their way into Britain from around AD 410, moving up from Kent into East Anglia by AD 500. Some of the distinctive round flint towers for which East Anglia is well known date from the Anglo-Saxon period, and can be found in all the countries surrounding the North Sea. Their religious administrative centre was based at North Elmham in Norfolk, where a cathedral was built and trade and the arts flourished across the region.

By the ninth century, the country was divided into the four kingdoms of Northumbria, Mercia, East Anglia and Wessex. A variety of Viking and Danish invasions impacted on the region, with the Danes dominating for nearly 200 years. Apart from contributing their fair hair and blue eyes to the local population, the Danes left many place names – the most obvious those ending in *by, dale, holme, toft, thorpe* or *gate* (meaning street).

The Danes were driven out of East Anglia in 917 and East Anglia became part of the kingdom of the West Saxons. Danish raiding began again in the late tenth century, with the whole of eastern England surrendering in 1013. When the Danish King Canute also became King of Norway in 1028, England became part of a wide empire, centred on the North Sea, undoubtedly benefiting the east of England. By the time of the Norman invasion in 1066, East Anglia had become one of the most densely populated and wealthiest areas of Britain.

Despite the general economic slump following the plagues of the fourteenth century, East Anglia remained wealthy due to its position as the centre of the wool and textiles trades. Although it would be inaccurate to say this remained constant across the whole region at all times; it was undoubtedly a dominant economic force for several centuries. By the early 1800s the spread of industrialization combined with agricultural depressions meant the north of England became a focus for work and trade opportunities, and East Anglia declined in status.

Although many traditional occupations have dwindled across East Anglia, the region still retains a distinctive rural character which complements the growing urban areas and successfully incorporates many of the benefits of a modern age. As a result, the region manages to maintain a healthy balance between old and new, whilst retaining a timeless quality.

2.1 Cambridgeshire

Cambridgeshire is bounded by Lincolnshire to the north, Norfolk and Suffolk to the east, by Essex and Hertfordshire to the south and Bedfordshire, Huntingdonshire and Northamptonshire to the west. Although Cambridgeshire has rivers and canals it is the only one of the four counties with no coastline. The principal rivers are the Ouse, the Cam and the Nene. The north of the county, including the Isle of Ely and part of the Great Bedford Level, was once submerged in marsh. This was turned into farmland when the Fens were drained via a network of canals. The vale of the Cam stretched from this area to the south-west and traditionally supported a large number of dairy farms.

Cambridgeshire has built a reputation for resistance to invaders. One of those was Hereward the Wake who used the Isle of Ely as a base against the Norman invaders. The county has also been notable for its strong history of non-conformity and influential and interesting characters such Oliver Cromwell and William Lax, who never gave a single lecture during the thirty-two years he occupied the Chair of Astronomy and Geometry at Cambridge between 1795 and 1837.

South Cambridgeshire covers 250 square miles around the city of Cambridge, one of the leading academic centres in the world. Cambridge was founded when the Romans built a town by the River Cam on a site previously settled by an Iron Age tribe. The Romans were followed by the Saxons and Normans and the remains of the stone castle built after the Norman Conquest still stands adjacent to the Shire Hall and county record office. The Romans planted vines in this area and it remains one of the main producers of British wine today.

The northern part of Cambridgeshire is mostly Fenland extending from the Isle of Ely to the Wash and contains some of the richest soil in England. Before the Fens were drained (see agriculture) this was a land of mist, marshes and bogs, with villages and towns appearing out of the landscape on small islands inhabited by people who lived on fish and waterfowl. It was this

Old Fen watermill at Isleham.

landscape that has given rise to numerous legends of web-footed people, ghosts and witchcraft.

The city of Ely lies at the heart of the Fens. It was once known as *Elge* or *Elig* (eel island) because of the number of eels in the surrounding waters. It was founded as a monastery by St Etheldreda, who remained abbess there until her death in 679. Work began in the present Cathedral in 1081 and was completed in 1189, with the Cathedral set within the walls of the monastery. The tourist information centre is housed in what was once the home of Oliver Cromwell.

Huntingdon is renowned as birthplace of Oliver Cromwell in 1599. He attended the town's Grammar School, which Samuel Pepys also attended at a later date. Cromwell was Member of Parliament for Huntingdon in the Parliament of 1629, was made a Justice of the Peace in 1630 and moved to St Ives in Cambridgeshire the next year. Rising to power as a military commander in the Civil War he was appointed Lord Protector in 1653 and ran the country until his death in 1658.

Peterborough, in the north of the county, is Cambridgeshire's second city, dating back to the Bronze Age. Although a cathedral city it is also a new town (designated in 1967) thereby combining modern development and expansion with a historic centre.

2.2 Essex

Essex was one of the early English kingdoms, formed by the East Saxons who settled here in the fifth century in an area previously occupied by a Celtic tribe known as the Trinobantes, or Trinovantes (meaning battle-spearers, or battle-stabbers), who are known to have been living here when the Romans invaded. The county occupies an important maritime position along the North Sea and the estuary of the River Thames. Almost a peninsula, it is bounded on the north by the River Stour; the east by the North Sea; the south by the River Thames and the west by the River Lea.

Before the boundary changes of the twentieth century which transferred some parishes such as North Woolwich to neighbouring counties, Essex was the tenth largest county in England. Its strong Saxon links are illustrated by the fact that when Harold, the last Saxon king, was defeated by the Normans at the Battle of Hastings, his body was buried in the church at Waltham.

Although famous for its ports, Essex remained predominantly agricultural until the mid-twentieth century. In 1700, around two-thirds of the population,

Former farmhouses by the green in the hamlet of Bentfield End in Essex.

(92,000 to 97,000 people), lived in the 370 parishes outside towns and cities. Around a quarter of these parishes had less than 100 inhabitants. Even those who lived in larger parishes were spread out amongst several hamlets.

Historian G F Bosworth, in his history of the county published in 1922, described West Ham, East Ham, Leyton, Walthamstow, Barking, Ilford, Wanstead and Woodford as having retained their own distinct rural identity with green fields, pretty gardens, farms and orchards until the end of the nineteenth century, but that they were now known as 'London-over-the-Border'. He went on to say that now 'there are countless miles of streets with commonplace houses of identical pattern'.

2.3 Norfolk

The Norfolk motto of 'Do Different' ideally describes a distinctive Norfolk character. It is bounded by Cambridgeshire, Lincolnshire and Suffolk, with the north and east sides bordered by the sea, and the west by the Fens. Sand dunes and salt marshes cover large sections of the ninety mile coastline. The south-west of the county, between the county capital of Norwich and the border with Suffolk, is effectively a plateau, distinguished by its sandy heath lands and dotted by old market towns such as Diss and Wymondham.

The valleys of the Yare and Bure are well known for their reed swamps and the Broads, lakes that resulted from medieval peat cutting. The coast stretches from Great Yarmouth in the east to Cromer on the edge of the county and west to Sheringham, Hunstanton and beyond. Substantial stretches are now under the care of the National Trust, including the highest point at West Runton.

Norwich, a 'fine city', has an intricate network of winding streets and historic buildings. Once an important centre of the wool trade, Norwich has over thirty surviving medieval churches. A well known local saying claims that at one time Norwich had 'a church for every Sunday and a pub for every day of the year'. By the fourteenth century Norfolk was one of the wealthiest and most highly populated counties in England, with wide ranging trading links with other parts of Europe.

The county's importance financially, politically and spiritually is indicated by the shrine at Little Walsingham in north Norfolk which attracted pilgrims from all over the country and abroad in the Middle Ages. Norfolk retained its influential position until the nineteenth century, when industrialization and agricultural depressions led to a decline in population in rural areas and many traditional trades and industries.

2.4 Suffolk

Miles Jebb, in his history of the county, describes Norfolk and Suffolk as being brother and sister with Norfolk having 'a stronger and more masculine identity, derived from its longer coastline and greater distance from London' whilst Suffolk 'presents more feminine and gentle charms'. Situated between the rivers Waveney in the north and Stour in the south, Suffolk is distinguished by shallow valleys and heath land. Ness Point in Lowestoft is the most easterly point in Suffolk and, therefore, the most easterly point of England. Ness Point is also the site of Suffolk's first commercial wind turbine, producing electricity for 1,500 homes.

The eighth largest county in England, Suffolk is bordered by Norfolk to the north, the North Sea to the east, Essex to the south and Cambridgeshire to the west. It has produced probably the finest collection of artists, writers, poets and composers in England such as John Constable, Thomas Gainsborough and Benjamin Britten.

There is much evidence of Stone Age occupation, with the flint tools uncovered in Pakefield being 200,000 years older than any previous finds. The discovery of the seventh century ship burial at Sutton Hoo is one of the most important Saxon discoveries in the country. The remains of a coastal fortress, built in the county by the Romans, survive at Burgh Castle (now part of Norfolk). It is one of eleven recorded Roman forts between the Wash and the Solent, part of a chain built to protect the coast from Saxon raiders. Its large circular bastions, designed to support the weight of the Roman artillery, and the three remaining walls are an impressive sight. The Romans abandoned it in around AD 408 and some 200 years later the Irish missionary St Fursey founded a monastery within its walls. It guards the Waveney and Yare at what was the head of an important waterway running into East Anglia.

The capture and execution of King Edmund by the Danes in AD 870 is generally believed to have occurred in Hoxne. According to legend Goldbrook Bridge gained its name because Edmund hid under it while retreating from the Danes. He was betrayed when a bridal couple saw the reflection of his gold spurs in the water. Since then there has been a tradition of bad luck for any couples crossing the bridge on their wedding day. His body is believed to have been taken to Bury, which was subsequently renamed Bury St Edmund's. King Edmund was subsequently considered the patron saint of England until St George replaced him under Richard I.

Hoxne's other claim to fame occurred in 1992 when what became known as the Hoxne hoard of nearly 15,000 Roman coins and 200 other gold and silver objects was discovered buried in a chest. The find is one of the largest hoards of Roman treasure ever found and is now on display at the British Museum.

Many important places, politically and commercially, can be found across the county, such as Orford where Henry II built a castle between 1165 and 1173 to defend the area against seaborne invaders. Close to the Fens is Mildenhall, the largest parish in Suffolk, and once a port for the area of west Suffolk lying along the River Lark. A remarkable hoard of Saxon silver was discovered here in 1946 and is now on display at the British Museum. Nearby Lakenheath is perhaps most famous today for being the home of the US Air Force.

Hoxne Church in Suffolk in the 1940s.

Suffolk is particularly rich in thatched, half timbered and colour-washed buildings dating from the Middle Ages onwards. This colour is known as Suffolk Pink, and believed to have originally been made with a mixture of ox blood and whitewash. The craft of decorated plasterwork called pargetting still adorns thousands of buildings.

Chapter Three

WORK, TRADE AND COMMERCE (OR HOW EAST ANGLIA RULED THE WORLD)

Although work and trade often share common themes across the region, some aspects are either unique to, or dominant within, a particular county or area. It would, however, be impossible to feature all. So, taking the counties individually, what follows are the most influential, and the impact of technological and social changes on patterns of work and the lives of the people involved in them.

3.1 Agriculture

Agricultural work dominated the working life of the vast majority of people in East Anglia in the past. As the terms 'farmer' and 'labourer' are frequently used as generic terms, the range, complexity of skills and types of work undertaken can become hidden. A farmer might be anything from the owner of several hundred acres or a tenant of a small holding, whilst large numbers of householders often farmed a few acres for their own use as well as working for other people. People described as labourers might be also anything from a farmer, yeoman or husbandman to a farm bailiff or cowman. This is illustrated in the 1815 settlement examination of William Gilham. Although he was hired as a servant in husbandry to Thomas Chaplin of Foulsham in Norfolk, his master was also a brandy merchant. During the time Gilham worked for Chaplin he spent a couple of weeks hoeing turnips for Mr Buck of Guist with his master's permission. His examination also gives a glimpse of wider concerns, as Gilham describes how, 'being fearful of being impress into the Sea Service', he went away with his master's consent for about a fortnight.

The world of agricultural work was never static. Drainage in the Fens transformed parts of seventeenth century Cambridgeshire. Enclosure affected all counties, although some, like Cambridgeshire, adopted it relatively late and opposition to the loss of common land and the introduction of machinery was often violent.

Despite some major agricultural depressions in the early 1800s and the abolition of the Corn Laws in 1846, which opened competition to other countries, farming generally advanced. Improved methods and imperial expansion opening up markets, meant British agriculture entered a period of prosperity lasting to the 1880s. This coincided with the growth of the railways, and their impact in being able to transport goods cheaply and efficiently. Nevertheless, the life of the farm worker was still characterized by hard work, low pay and poverty, until wages were substantially increased after the Second World War.

From the end of the nineteenth century, and up to the First World War, farming was in decline, due to a mixture of cheap imports from other countries, several years of bad weather and poor harvests. Although farming had a brief resurgence during the war these factors exacerbated a population movement away from rural areas that had begun in the early 1800s. The census returns for Essex illustrate this and tell us that the number of people employed in agriculture fell by 56 per cent between 1861 and 1931.

By 1991, less than 1 per cent of the population were farmers or agricultural labourers. Nevertheless, whilst agriculture in East Anglia no longer has such a big part in the working lives of people; it has changed and diversified, and still plays a vital economic role in the region.

3.1.1 Cambridgeshire

The Domesday Survey makes many references to the production of wheat, malt and honey in the county, whilst barley for malt was grown in large quantities in the south in the sixteenth century. By the 1700s Cambridgeshire still had a mixed pastoral economy of crops, cattle and sheep rearing, benefiting from the rich soil in the north. This gradually gave way to arable farming, with Saffron, a crocus used for dyestuffs, being extensively cultivated in the eighteenth century.

Samuel Lewis's *Topographical Gazetteer* of 1831 describes the county as producing an 'abundant supply of corn', with the Fenland area being particularly productive, especially for oats, hemp and flax. Dairy farming was also predominant around the south Cambridgeshire parishes of Soham,

Littleport and Willingham, with the butter they sold in London markets called 'Cambridge' butter.

Cambridge had become one of the country's most celebrated commercial centres by the thirteenth century, hosting the renowned Stourbridge Fair held annually on Stourbridge Common. This ran until 1834, attracting people from as far as the Low Countries, and trading in everything from silk to hops. At its peak it was the largest fair in Europe and was believed to be the inspiration for John Bunyan's Vanity Fair in *Pilgrim's Progress*.

Farmers in several villages were initially unwilling to support Parliamentary enclosure with some, like Soham, never becoming formally enclosed at all. Littleport was the site of riots in 1831 which resulted in several deaths, when labourers from Ely and Littleport, facing rising unemployment, low wages and soaring food prices, attacked houses and people in the area. Five of the rioters where hanged and buried in a common grave in St Mary's Church in Littleport and are commemorated in a plaque there.

The late nineteenth century saw much land put down to pasture and some practically abandoned. Market gardening thrived from the late nineteenth century, with some, who produced seeds for farmers, being converted into garden centres in the twentieth century. Large flocks of sheep were still kept, partly for fertilizing the ground, and some landowners specialized in rarer breeds such as merino sheep. However, the keeping of livestock gradually declined in the twentieth century.

Other crops were introduced from the 1930s, including mustard and sugar beet. Arable farming revived in the late twentieth century with barley often being the main crop in areas producing cereals. Market towns like St Ives in the west of Cambridgeshire were of vital importance in facilitating trade. A market still takes place there every Monday, providing a continuous link back to those of the Middle Ages.

3.1.2 The Fens

For generations much of the Fens were only accessible by boat, with the Isle of Ely taking its name from the eels filling the surrounding waters which formed a principal part of the diet of the monks based there. When Hilgay was recorded in the *Domesday Book* as one of only two settlements in the Norfolk Fens, it was a low hill rising out of surrounding marshland.

The stagnant waters of the Fens gave off an obnoxious vapour which was believed to induce a form of malarial fever known as Fen ague. In the nineteenth century Fenland inhabitants began taking opium based medicines to relieve the pains of this illness. This was so prevalent that one Wisbech based pharmacist was recorded as keeping over forty gallons of laudanum in stock in 1894.

The Romans attempted to control this landscape by building large causeways of oak trunks, chalk and gravel. Yet, even they could get lost in its fog bound watery landscape, with the historian Dio Cassius complaining that the inhabitants were almost amphibious, standing for days with only their heads protruding from the water when surrounded.

Throughout the Middle Ages large areas were reclaimed for agriculture, with much of the work undertaken by the monasteries. Increasingly, more ambitious landowners believed that draining the Fens was the way to improve agriculture. Sir Cornelius Vermuyden embarked on the first major drainage scheme when he was employed by the Duke of Bedford in 1630 to drain the southern Fenland, beginning with 20,000 acres near Whittlesey to bypass the Great Ouse. Resuming work after the Civil War he cut the New Bedford River parallel to the first. These two drains run side by side for more than thirteen miles and still provide the basic drainage for much of the Fenland. The strip of land between them is called the Ouse Washes, and is never more than 1,000 yards wide. This is deliberately allowed to flood during the winter so the fields on either side can stay dry.

The River Great Ouse at Littleport, centre of the Fens drainage schemes.

There was however; considerable local opposition. Some Fen dwellers whose way of life was threatened, attacked the Dutch drainage workers, notoriously placing their women at the front to deflect retaliation. When this occurred in Soham and Wicken in the 1630s and Swaffham Prior in the 1650s, such was local sympathy that few local justices, clergy, parish officers or men called out from nearby villages were willing to assist the authorities in restraining them.

The soil exposed by drainage was mostly peat and, as it shrank, the ground level fell. Over the years it became necessary to pump rainwater from the fields up into the rivers and, as in Holland, wind pumps took on this task. Steam pumps were introduced in the 1800s to drain the Fens and marshes, replacing the many wind pumps.

3.1.3 Essex

The nature of Essex prior to industrialization can be illustrated by remarks made by Daniel Defoe, author of *Gulliver's Travels* when he toured the east of England in 1722:

> The product of all this part of the country is corn, as that of the marshy feeding grounds mentioned above is grass, where their chief business is breeding of calves, which I need not say are the best and fattest, and the largest veal in England, if not in the world; and, as an instance, I ate part of a veal or calf, fed by the late Sir Josiah Child at Wanstead, the loin of which weighed above thirty pounds, and the flesh exceeding white and fat.

Essex saw some of the greatest militancy between farm workers and their employers in the struggle for improved pay and working conditions. Early sympathies were shown when the villages of Greensted and High Layer gave homes to the Tolpuddle Martyrs from Dorset after their convictions for forming a trade union in 1834 were commuted in 1837.

One of the key figures in the fight for better conditions later in the century was Charles Jay, a farmer based at Coldham Hall, near Coggeshall. Determined to improve the welfare of farm workers he collaborated with Joseph Arch, a Methodist lay preacher, in working for the Essex branch of the National Agricultural Labourers Union (NALU). Farm labourers flocked to join the union, generating hostility among landowners, who formed defence associations in response.

In February 1874 labourers at Exning near Stowmarket demanded a rise of one shilling a week. The Newmarket Farmers' Defence Association responded with a lock-out which spread into Essex, resulting in around 10,000 men being locked out, with many evicted from their tied cottages. The lock out ended on 27 July as the union and its supporters were unable to continue supplying the financial support needed. Despite an attempt to form a land company to purchase land on which to settle labourers, the union fractured, membership fell and the movement for the unionization of farm labourers all but died in the county for many years.

The next major dispute in Essex occurred in 1914 in the Helions Bumpstead area when local farmer, Richard Ruffle, gave an ultimatum to ten workers who had joined a newly formed union to quit or lose their jobs. Within weeks, other farmers followed suit and conflict escalated, resulting in a strike involving over 800 workers from nearby villages in Essex as well as some in Cambridgeshire and Suffolk. As the dispute spread and violence flared a wide range of groups and individuals began to support the labourers. The strike ended with the outbreak of war, with the farmers agreeing to some of the wage demands.

3.1.4 Norfolk

Much of the soil in Norfolk is rich and in the growing of crops and grazing of sheep and cattle, lay the foundations of Norfolk's prosperity from at least the Domesday survey. Following the gradual enclosures of open fields, there were innovations such as the rotation of crops, the use of marl to reduce acidity in the soil, the growing of turnips as winter feed for cattle and to clear the land for cultivation, the growing of clover, long leases for tenant farmers and bigger farms, and improvements in drainage and livestock through selective breeding. Thomas Coke of Norfolk at Holkham and Turnip Townshend of Raynham are probably the most well known innovators in farming in England, influenced by methods already used in the Low Countries.

Norfolk did, however, suffer during the agricultural depressions of the nineteenth century. In 1816, when the war with France had ended, food was scarce and riots broke out in the west of the county. The *Norfolk Chronicle* reported the first machine breaking case in May of that year at Hockham when four labourers were indicted for having "riotously assembled with 100 other persons'. Farm workers also participated in the riots and machine breaking of the 1820s and 1830s.

Mustard farming has become identified with Norfolk through Colman's Mustard Company, one of the country's oldest existing food brands. Now owned by Unilever, it was founded in 1814 by Jeremiah Colman, a flour miller, who began making mustard at Bawburgh before moving to Stoke Holy Cross in 1823. Jeremiah James Colman moved the firm to Carrow on the edge of Norwich in 1862, where it was well served by road, rail and river, and from where the firm still operates today.

By 1880 the day of the great Norfolk estates, supported by the rents of tenant farmers had arrived. Today, Norfolk is still a strongly agricultural area, combining traditional crops and livestock, with new twists and variations on those from the past. For example, Heacham in west Norfolk is the home of a world famous lavender farm at Caley Mill, where 150 varieties of lavender are cultivated and an annual lavender festival is held each July.

3.1.5 Suffolk
Suffolk is famous for its horses, with the oldest breed of heavy horse in the world being the Suffolk Punch, which originated in at least the fifteenth century. Known for its docile temperament it is still in use on farms today.

Crops traditionally grown in the county have been wheat, oats, beans, peas, turnips, carrots, cabbage and potatoes. Rabbits, geese and turkeys have also

Ipswich Cattle Market in the 1920s.

been reared on an extensive scale, whilst hops and hemp have been cultivated on a small scale over the centuries, and sheep, bred for their wool, have also formed a large percentage of farming stock within the county.

Within the last century Suffolk has adapted to circumstances, for example by being at the forefront of the sugar beet industry. However, although Suffolk still has around four-fifths of its land devoted to agriculture, only a small percentage of the population works in the agricultural sector.

3.2 Finding out More

Many official records do not give a true reflection of women's occupations. The census, for instance, was designed to include information in relation to the 'head of the household', usually a man. Therefore many women, especially the married, are recorded without any occupation even though their work was an integral part of the day-to-day running of farms, smallholdings and other businesses. The same is also true for older children in a family, who may simply be recorded as a 'scholar'. Nevertheless, there are countless sources which tell us more about the working life of all our ancestors either directly or indirectly. What follows is a general flavour of those sources of use in highlighting your ancestors agricultural past.

Details of tenancies and sales of farms, farm land, and mills and other buildings can be found amongst estate records, deeds and manorial records. Local authority records also include relevant information about land and property ownership and tenancy.

Sales particulars from local estate agents such as those of Bidwell and Son, held at Cambridge Record Office, physically describe farms, mills and allotments, including their acreage, types of produce and so on. An example from the large collection at Norfolk Record Office from Savills Estate Agents is the one for a dairy farm known as Holly Lodge Farm in Bergh Apton. This gives a valuation of the crops grown and describes the house, its farm buildings and fifty-two acres of land.

Other information can be found in the Valuation Office Survey of 1910, otherwise known as the Lloyd George Domesday. This assessed the value of land and property across the country. The original assessments and maps are held in The National Archives, but copies of the valuations can be found in local offices.

Parish records such as churchwardens' and overseers' accounts and poor law papers frequently include references to the ownership or tenancy of properties. One of the criteria for gaining a settlement in a parish was to have owned or leased property over a certain rateable value. Thus when Mary Hall, of St Clement in Ipswich, was examined as to her settlement by parish officials in 1799, she stated her husband Daniel had occupied a farm in Battisford and Ringshall and a tenement in Battisford in Suffolk, 'in which he lodged & which she hath heard he was the proprietor of'.

A revealing insight into how young children were used in agricultural labour can be seen in a newspaper report on the death of 8 year old Joseph Gowen of Butley in Suffolk, who died of an apoplexy while employed as a labourer to frighten birds off a corn field. Many examples of accidents also feature in local papers, such as the entry in the transcripts to the *Beccles and Bungay Weekly News* on GENUKI of a report on Frederick Downing who lost his thumb and three fingers in an accident in 1862 while working on a steam sawing machine.

An entry in the card indexes to newspaper reports at Bury St Edmunds record office, referring to the assault on gamekeeper William Otley in January 1796, gives us a glimpse into other aspects of rural life. As does the conviction of Edward High, of Salthouse in Norfolk, for night poaching in April 1891 and the diary entry of Parson Woodforde in 1786 which recorded that:

> Poor Tom Twaites of Honingham who was beat by the Poachers at Mr Townshends the other day is lately dead of the Wounds he then recd.

Registers frequently include comments on local and social events. One such case is the burial register for Thompson, Norfolk in 1776. A reference to the death of 12 year old Daniel Jonas of Thimblethorpe [Themelthorpe] has a condemnatory tone as it describes how he froze to death while driving cattle to London because his master had sent him out in the cold without proper clothing.

In most cases little survives in the way of individual employment records for agricultural workers, except perhaps on some of the larger estates. Very occasionally parish registers, census returns and birth, marriage and death certificates will include an employer's details.

Details of individuals' work, what they were paid, work and social conditions can, however, be found in some parish records, particularly in the settlement examinations taken to establish where someone 'belonged'. For example, in Thetford St Peter in 1816, Robert Clarke described how he let himself, three weeks after Michaelmas 1799, to Robert Barnard Esq., of Great Ellingham Hall, Norfolk until the Michaelmas following. When he left his service in 1800 he received two guineas and a half wages. The following year he received three pounds wages, and an extra shilling for driving the stock from Hopton to Sisland.

References to the places workers lived in parish registers, census records and certificates of births, marriage and death will provide addresses, although that is often just the village name. By using maps and trade directories it is possible to identify likely local employers and the range of occupations in that place. For instance, in Littleport, Cambridgeshire, around thirty farmers and their addresses are listed in an 1850 trade directory. Farmers and landowners will also appear in parish rate lists, electoral rolls, poll books and the land tax assessments compiled between 1692 and 1832.

Both Hodskinson's 1783 and Bryant's 1824–35 maps of Suffolk have been reproduced in A4 booklets by Larks Press. Both can be accessed at the county record offices along with numerous ordnance surveys, estate plans and charts of the river.

Tithe and enclosure maps and their accompanying awards and apportionments include the names of owners and occupiers. Most enclosure maps date from the early 1800s, but tend to include fewer names. They will, however, list the many small to middling farmers who took the opportunity to buy plots of land, some of which they had farmed as tenants.

Many references to land ownership and tenancies appear in wills as when Edward Lant left a parcel of 'Fen or Marsh Ground in Ramsey in a Fen or place commonly called the Gow late part of the Gow Common' when he died in 1840.

Newspapers commonly carried advertisements or items about farms for sale or to let. One such report in the *Norfolk Chronicle* about an auction in August 1899 stated Mr Robert Borrett sold 170 acres of land in the Moulton St Michael area with the wheat and barley still growing on it. This went on to say the crops were included because of the scarcity of labour 'a circumstance unprecedented in Norfolk'.

The records of the *Bedford Level Corporation*, which drained the Fenland, include a registry of deeds and petitions from the mid-seventeenth century onwards regarding improvements of drains and access across land. These are held at Cambridge Record Office and include numerous references to local inhabitants. In 1826 for example, a John Shinn was accused of illegally retaining the keepership of the Brandon river staunch, although a Thomas Cooper had been elected to the office.

Other records relating to leases in the Fens include a listing at the Norfolk Record Office for the Wormegay Drainage Commissioners regarding banks let, and rents received, 1815–19 with a note of conditions of letting which can be found amongst the parish council records for Wormegay.

Upheavals such as machine breaking and swing riots were widely reported in the press and those tried and convicted appear in court records, both locally and nationally. For instance, a listing found amongst the Petty Sessions records held at Essex Record Office describes 'divers tumults and riots' that had taken place in the Braintree area in 1830.

3.3 Bringing it to Life

The old farm buildings at the Farmland Museum at Denny Abbey near Waterbeach have been renovated and tell the story of village life and Cambridgeshire farming up to modern times.

Dating from 1831, the Stretham Old Engine near Wicken is the last of the ninety steam pumping engines installed throughout the Fens to replace 800

Farm building at the Farmland Museum and Denny Abbey near Waterbeach.

windmills. It remained working until 1925, and was kept on standby until the 1940s.

Prickwillow Drainage Museum has been in continuous use as a pumping station since 1831 and has a unique collection of large engines associated with the Fens drainage.

The March and District Museum tells the story of the people and history of March and the surrounding area, including a working forge.

The Ashdon Village Collection in Essex is a museum of village life with interesting displays of agriculture, the home, shopping and entertainment.

Dedham Vale on the border of Essex and Suffolk is often referred to as 'Constable Country' because of its association with the artist. Many surviving buildings like Flatford Mill and Willy Lott's cottage are immortalized in his works, providing both a contemporary representation and physical reminder.

Gressenhall Farm and Workhouse Museum, Norfolk, is a museum of rural life and traditional farm with rare breed animals.

Denver Sluice was originally built in 1651 by Vermuyden as part of the Fens drainage scheme and is still in use today.

The Museum of East Anglian Life in Stowmarket, Suffolk includes a wide array of displays and artefacts relating to rural life.

Close to Wortham churchyard on the Redgrave road is a memorial to the tithe wars of the 1930s, when farmers resisted paying a tax to support the church. Richard Rash and his wife, Dorothy Wallace, refused to pay in 1933, leading a march of farm workers to the rectory in protest. Rash then used a guard of Fascist Black Shirts in a failed attempt to prevent the bailiffs seizing his goods in lieu of payment.

The insights of a local smallholder into the rural economy of a Cambridgeshire village can be found in *A Peasant's Voice to Landowners by John Denson of Waterbeach* (Cambridge Record Society, 1991). This is a collection of letters sent to local newspapers by Denson, which were subsequently gathered into a pamphlet with additional facts and opinions. Their publication also includes most of a 1795 history of Waterbeach.

Parson Woodforde's diaries provide numerous accounts of work and life in a rural village in Norfolk, as when he describes employing a rat-catcher in 1782:

> Cobb of Mattishall, a Rat-Catcher … came to my House this morning by Order, and I engaged with him for to kill all my Rats at one Guinea Per Annum and likewise kill all my Mice … He is to come as

often as there is an Occasion for him – And to be kept in Victuals and drink.

Norfolk born George Edwards (1850–1933) rose from a life of poverty to become a farm workers' union pioneer, an MP, and gain a knighthood. In his autobiography, *From Crow-scaring to Westminster* (London, 1922) he describes how, as a boy of 6, he went to work for a shilling a week scaring crows:

> During the wheat cutting I made bonds for the binders. There were no reaping machines in those days, the corn all having to be cut by the scythe … At the conclusion of the harvest they would have what they called a gleaners' frolic.

The allotment movement forms an evolutionary link in the history of agriculture. Originally enabling people to grow their own food, especially in urban areas, they also played a vital role in food production in wartime. A recent publication on the history called *Norfolk Allotments – the plot so far* describes the social history of allotment provision nationally, with special reference to Norfolk, including thirty case studies.

Walberswick windmill in the 1920s.

Oral histories like the Suffolk Voices project provide first hand descriptions of the experiences of people in many trades and occupations including farming. The job of a miller is one of those associated with agriculture, but not just a part of it. Mills have been an integral part of part of the regions landscape for at least 800 years, and were still a major industry into the late nineteenth century. Today our region sees the growth of a new type of mill; the wind turbines used for generating electricity. Still controversial, many supporters see them as a variation on a traditional sight in the regions landscape. Some working mills still remain, whilst others have found new uses as tourist attractions, museums, heritage sites or holiday accommodation. A few worth visiting are:

Bourne in south Cambridgeshire is home to Britain's oldest surviving post mill dating from the early seventeenth century.

Townsford mill in Halstead in Essex is a three-storey white weatherboard watermill built in the 1700s. It formed part of the infrastructure of the Courtauld textiles company founded by Huguenot refugees.

Thorrington tide mill, built in the early nineteenth century, is the only remaining tide mill in Essex, and one of very few surviving anywhere in East Anglia. Fully restored, the wheel can be run for guided groups.

The famous tower windmill at Thaxted was built in 1804 and remained in working order until 1907. Now restored, it contains a rural life museum. Thaxted is also famous for Morris dancing, one of England's oldest traditional folk dance forms. It was revived here in 1911 by the vicar's wife, Miriam Noel, and an annual gathering of Morris dancers from all over England is held every spring.

The windmill at Stansted Mountfitchet was built in 1797 and is one of the best preserved tower mills in the country.

Upminster smock mill was built in 1803 and retains much of its original equipment including grinding stones.

Amongst the many Norfolk mills worth visiting is the windmill at Great Bircham. Dating from 1846 it has been fully restored and is open to the public.

The post mill at Saxtead Green, Suffolk is one of the finest windmills remaining in England. Still in working order, it continued in commercial use until 1947.

Pakenham is the only village in England to still have both a windmill and watermill in working order.

The Herringfleet wind pump dates from 1820 and is the last survivor of the old style Broadland windpumps, with cloth-spread sails and a boat-shaped cap, turned manually by a tailpole and winch. The water is lifted by an external scoopwheel. It remained in regular use until the early 1950s.

3.4 Coast and Waterways

The coast, rivers and waterways of East Anglia have their own special place in the lives of our ancestors through work, transportation and leisure. What follows under each county is a closer look at some of the key trades and occupations. Fishing is a dominant theme across the region and no mention of trade could ignore the many thriving ports which acted as a focal point for people moving in and out, as well as the transport of goods and numerous trades and occupations.

Unofficial commerce such as piracy and smuggling undoubtedly contributed to East Anglia's economic life, and was possibly of greater importance to some towns and villages than fishing. The Suffolk coast was very popular for smuggling as it was less well defended than Essex or Kent. In 1224 for example, residents in Orford were requested to assist the Keeper of the Shore to prevent smuggling, whilst records at Ipswich Record Office include a 1550/1 order from the High Admiral to the Vice-Admiral in Norfolk and Suffolk requesting he:

> ... take a view of all ships and seamen in his area ... and to give order for arrest of English, Scottish or other sea rovers and pirates.

Suffolk was also home to two of the most famous women pirates of the sixteenth century; Lady Mary Killigrew from Woolverstone and Mrs Peter Lambert of Aldeburgh in Suffolk. By 1626 the incumbent of Santon Downham was writing in his diary of the Dunkirkers 'who troubled our seas', whilst Captain Francis Sydenham was sent to Orfordness in 1630 in an attempt to repel the groups of pirates based at Dunkirk in France attacking defenceless shipping.

Tea, brandy, silk and lace were the staple commodities in the eighteenth century with much large scale smuggling organized by traders in the Flemish ports, who covered their activities with legal trading. People at all levels of society are known to have colluded with smuggling through either a mixture of self-interest or intimidation. Parson Woodforde recorded in his diary how, in March 1777, 'Andrews the Smuggler brought me this night about 11 o'clock a bagg of Hyson Tea 6 Pd weight'; and in December 1786 'Had another Tub of Gin and another of the best Conias Brandy brought me this Evening'.

Edward Cox Tooby, a Customs and Excise supervisor, was seriously injured in 1816 when a cargo of contraband was landed at Caister just north of Great Yarmouth. When the six smugglers captured were bailed at the local court, these records indicate a certain amount of tolerance towards their activities, as local people stood surety for those on trial. A later newspaper report in February 1822 described how a boat landed eighty tubs of gin and brandy on Snettisham beach where twenty or thirty horses and carts were waiting to move the goods. When excise officers seized the cargo part of it was rescued by the smugglers with the help of about 100 others.

Parish registers frequently include references to drowned sailors and lost ships, and, although not strictly occupational, lighthouses and lifeboats have played a crucial role in the lives of those who have lived and worked on the coast. The first brick lighthouse in England was built at Lowestoft Ness in 1676, guiding ships between Lowestoft and Winterton. The lighthouses at Orford, Southwold and Lowestoft are within a few miles of each other, and testament to the treacherous nature of that part of the coast. Perhaps not surprisingly, Lowestoft was the first place in Suffolk to have a specially designated lifeboat in 1801. A special 'Norfolk and Suffolk' lifeboat design was developed over the years, with an almost flat bottom, so it could operate amongst the moving sandbanks which are common along the coast.

Henry Blogg (1876–1954), was a lifeboat man for fifty-three years and coxswain of the Cromer lifeboat in Norfolk for thirty-eight, becoming the most decorated lifeboat man in England. During this time the Cromer boats saved 873 lives. Amongst the many awards he was given were the Royal National Lifeboat Institution gold medal three times, the silver medal four times as well as the George Cross and the British Empire Medal.

3.4.1 Cambridgeshire

Despite its lack of coastline Cambridgeshire does have a strong maritime connection because of its proximity to the Wash and the River Ouse. Wisbech was a port in medieval times and renowned for boatbuilding for several centuries. Although the port has declined in importance it still enjoys a shipping trade with Europe.

All the rivers in Cambridgeshire were famous for their fish, especially pike and eels, and there has been a long history of trade along the River Cam because of the lack of roads and inaccessibility of many Fenland villages.

Goods were transported in Fenland lighters which could carry twenty to twenty-five tons of cargo. These were about thirteen metres long with a beam of three metres, two central compartments with a cockpit at bow and stern connected by narrow side decks. By the end of the seventeenth century they were linked together in 'gangs' by ropes, chains or beams as it increased the amount of cargo which could be carried. Sails were sometimes used, but they mostly relied on horsepower. In Cambridge, horses had to walk along a raised causeway in the middle of the river between Quayside and Newnham, as there was no towpath.

The new canals of the eighteenth and early nineteenth centuries helped fuel the industrial revolution as an essential part of the transport network before the development of steam traction and the railway network system. Many canals which criss-cross the county were constructed for inland navigation through extending natural waterways, former Roman irrigation systems and as part of draining the Fens to reclaim the land (see Agriculture section). The New Bedford Canal was the main channel for barges passing from one end of the Ouse to the other. Other well used canals were the Outwell to Wisbech route and the canal running from Peterborough through Whittlesea Dyke to the old Nene River just below Benwick, then on to March.

Barges on the river at Outwell in the early twentieth century.

3.4.2 Essex

Essex has several low-lying islands at the mouths of its creeks and estuaries, with the larger ones of Mersea, Foulness and Canvey being inhabited. Fishing was a major industry in Essex for centuries; and it is probably most renowned for its oyster beds with Colchester, on the Colne estuary, still supporting oyster beds today. Despite the census returns recording a rise in the numbers of fishermen and women in the county from 1,349 to 8,000 between 1851 and 1901, fishing has suffered a major decline overall in the last 150 years, partially due to overseas competition. By 1931 the number of people in the trade in Essex had fallen to less than 3,000.

The Blackwater and Chelme Navigation also provided an essential water route through the county from the Thames via its estuary to Chelmsford. A number of ports in the county were very important until the switch to transporting fish by rail. Mistley adjacent to Manningtree, for example, thrived from 1705, when the River Stour was made navigable to Sudbury, until the coming of the railway in 1848. Coal was imported from Newcastle and timber from Norway, before goods were transferred to and from London. It is still in operation today, albeit in a small way.

Trade along the east coast from the River Humber to the south coast was dominated by the Thames sailing barges from the late 1780s to 1920s. Their shallow flat-bottomed hull made it possible for them to sail up the shallow creeks of Essex. These sailing barges delivered the huge amounts of hay and straw needed by the city for the thousands of horses used for transport. Essex, and Maldon in particular, evolved a special variety of barge called the 'stackie' designed to be shallow and wide for sailing with a haystack on deck. The Ipswich barges specialized in carrying flour and malting barley, with many owned by the flour millers Cranfield Brothers of Ipswich. Barges also carried timber, stone, sand, cement, ballast, bricks, oilcake, oil and plastics. After the First World War barge building was in decline. The last wooden barge built was the *Cabby* launched at Rochester in 1928 and the final steel barge was launched from Mistley in Essex in 1930.

Barking was the most important fishing port in Essex, mainly because the Barking well-smack, invented in the early eighteenth century, enabled fishermen to bring their catch back alive to be sold. In the mid-nineteenth century there were 140 fishing smacks of forty to sixty tons. Another important port was Brightlingsea which was noted for its shipbuilding, oysters and sprats, whilst Felixstowe is the second largest container port in Europe dealing with around 2 million containers every year.

Harwich had a considerable deep-sea fishing trade and the opening of the Royal Navy Yard in Harwich in 1657 encouraged a flourishing shipbuilding industry in the town for more than 200 years. Men like Sir Anthony Deane produced ships for the Navy and others, such as Joseph Graham in the 1800s, built for trade with the Baltic and other ports. Harwich is still a major port trading with the rest of Europe as well as home to one of the most important North Sea ferry terminals. Tilbury is another major container port, handling trade from all over the world, and an important cruise terminal.

3.4.3 Norfolk

Sheringham and Cromer on the coast of Norfolk epitomize the importance of the fishing industry to coastal areas, with Sheringham having over 150 fishing boats in the late nineteenth century. Many small villages like Cley-next-the-Sea in Norfolk were once busy commercial ports, mainly servicing the export of wool to the Netherlands. The nearby village of Salthouse was once a centre for salt production and storage, and its marshes are now one of the most important birdwatching sites along the north Norfolk coast.

The harbour at Wells-next-the-Sea.

Wells-next-the-Sea has been a working port since at least the thirteenth century, although the harbour now stands more than a mile from the sea. To prevent the harbour silting up altogether, Lord Leicester of Holkham Hall built an embankment cutting off around 600 acres of marshland. On the east coast is Great Yarmouth, famous for its port and fishing industry in the past, and now as a holiday resort.

King's Lynn on the Great Ouse, three miles inland from the Wash, was one of England's most important ports in medieval times. Links to the rest of the world can be seen in parish register entries, apprenticeships indexes and other records which refer to people from as far as Holland, Scotland and France. This can be seem in the town's numerous apprenticeship records as when Elias Fuller, the son of Ann Fuller a widow of Cauldecott in the county of Huntingdon, was apprenticed in 1662 to William Beddingham, a mariner of Lynn for seven years. Or, when Robert Syms of King's Lynn was apprenticed to his merchant father John in February 1653/54, it was agreed upon completion that he would become a free burgess of Lynn and also of the Company of Grocers Hall London and of the Society of Margarets [sic] trading into the 'East Land'.

King's Lynn viewed across the Wash from West Lynn.

When Daniel Defoe toured Norfolk in 1722 he commented on the 'trade and navigations' of Norwich, Great Yarmouth, King's Lynn, Wisbech, Wells-next-the-Sea, Burnham and Cley as well as smuggling activities along the coast:

> From Weyburn west lies Clye, where there are large salt-works and very good salt made which is sold all over the county, and sometimes sent to Holland and to the Baltic. From Clye we go to Marsham and to Wells... in which whereof there is a very considerable trade carried on with Holland for corn, which that part of the county is very full of. I say nothing of the great trade driven here from Holland, back again to England, because I take it to be a trade carried on with much less honesty than advantage, especially while the clandestine trade, or the art of smuggling was so much in practice: what it is now, is not to my present purpose.

For centuries, herring were gathered in their millions off the East Anglian coast every autumn, and from very early on were pickled or kippered. Coastal towns were assessed for their fisheries in terms of the number of herrings as early as the eleventh century, whilst in Elizabethan times Thomas Nash praised the herring for bringing prosperity to the coast of Norfolk and Suffolk.

Herring were still the basis of Great Yarmouth's prosperity in the nineteenth century when the author, Charles Dickens, commented on its all pervading smell when he stayed there in the 1840s. In the latter half of the century around sixty curing houses were occupied gutting, salting and spicing herrings to produce the kipper, and a local man, Mr Bishop, created a method which left the fish moist and full of flavour, so creating the Yarmouth bloater.

The Broads are stretches of shallow expanses of water formed in medieval times when peat was dug out to provide fuel. The majority lie in Norfolk to the east of Norwich, with a smaller percentage in Suffolk. These waterways have always been important transport routes, and now form Britain's finest wetland area. The traditional Broads boat was the wherry, a large single-sail vessel of shallow draught which transported cargoes of corn, coal and reed. As rail and road transport took over, the wherrys' original role was lost and many were converted for leisure use. The River Waveney, which forms a natural boundary between Suffolk and Norfolk was also widely used by

A wherry on the Broads at Reedham.

wherries and barges trading along its length, but is nowadays mainly used by pleasure boats.

3.4.4 Suffolk

The Suffolk coast stretches nearly forty miles along the North Sea from Lowestoft in the north to Felixstowe in the south. Although never a major shipbuilding region there were some places where it did flourish. The riverside town of Woodbridge for instance owes its affluence to the related industries of shipbuilding, sailcloth and rope-making. Slaughden just south of Aldeburgh was also once a prosperous shipbuilding centre. Although this declined as the river silted up, it is still popular with sailors. Suffolk's best known poet, George Crabbe, was born here in 1754 and often described his surroundings and the village's decline in his work. His solitary fisherman, Peter Grimes, became the subject of the opera composed by Aldeburgh based Benjamin Britten.

On the foreshore, north of Whapload Road in Lowestoft, several large anchors mark where the beach companies operated between 1762 and the 1940s. Their main business was recovering (known as swiping) anchors

A fish auction at Southwold harbour.

which had been lost from vessels waiting in the offshore anchorages for the wind to change so they could sail round Lowestoft Ness. The anchors would be subsequently sold to ships that needed a replacement.

Now well known as a holiday resort and yachting centre, Southwold has a long history as a fishing port, being named in the *Domesday Book*. Just inland is Blythburgh, a thriving port until the river silted up in the sixteenth century. The ports at Felixstowe, Lowestoft and Southwold were built in the early 1900s by the Coastal Development Company, which ran the Belle steamers which brought day trippers up to the coast from London Bridge.

Now the county town of Suffolk, Ipswich was originally a Saxon development, which became a thriving port and important ship-building centre. Ipswich is still used for both commercial shipping and pleasure craft. The striking Orwell Bridge carries Ipswich's eastern bypass across the docks and estuary and the nearby hamlet of Pin Mill on the south bank of the Orwell estuary is a popular yachting centre, always crowded with boats, including some old spritsail barges.

Although the rivers and streams of Suffolk supplied trout in large numbers in the past, it is the coast which is best known for fishing. Ports such as Dunwich, Walberswick, Southwold, Easton and Covehithe, specialized in

Ipswich Docks.

fishing for cod off Iceland as early as the sixteenth and seventeenth centuries, travelling in convoys of 100 to 200 vessels and making enormous profits. Lowestoft led the way in herring fishing as it was close to the shoals of fish and to Yarmouth, the centre of the herring trade. The seemingly limitless supply of herrings also attracted the Dutch fishing boats, although they were driven off in the seventeenth century.

In more recent times it was the Scots who came south in their trawlers. At the turn of the twentieth century between 400 and 500 Scottish fishing vessels based themselves in Lowestoft and Yarmouth for the herring season, supported by large numbers of Scots women and girls who came to gut and clean the fish. This trade was in its turn increased by the railway, which enabled the fish to be delivered to London quickly and efficiently. Over-fishing resulted in the collapse of the herring industry by the 1960s. Lowestoft today is still the base of fishing industry, albeit much reduced.

3.5 Finding out More

A book by Martin Wilcox due to be published in April 2009 entitled *Fishing and Fishermen: A Guide for Family Historians* (Pen & Sword Family History) describes the fishing industry and its records in depth.

Information can be found in a wide range of sources including census, parish registers, wills, business records and trade directories. In Norfolk, for example, the parish registers for Wells-next-the-Sea famously include entries to people from as far away as Iceland and Scotland, particularly in the burials. Local newspapers also reported fishing catches and carried advertisements from those in related trades.

People working as mariners, in shipbuilding or associated trades such as ship chandlers, shipbrokers, sailmakers and anchor or chain manufacturers frequently served apprenticeships. This was the case for William Hurn of Sheringham whose apprenticeship as a mariner to Henry Gooch of Great Yarmouth was arranged by the Sheringham parish authorities in 1779.

Ship owners were often merchants with trade interests and links to other parts of the country. William Crow, for example was a Norfolk born man who later lived in Halifax in Yorkshire, but owned part shares in the *Packet* built at Yarmouth in 1817, with a number of people based across the country. All local offices have a number of records relating to ship ownership, including registers of ships and fishing boats and log books. Some are held by borough or town archives and others in private collections. Very few are indexed in any detail but many of the record office catalogues give summary details which can include some names of ships, owners and masters.

Cambridgeshire Family History Society has a searchable online database to logged vessels in the port of Wisbech between 1860 and 1913, which are taken from documents held at Cambridge Record Office www.cfhs.org.uk/Clip

Essex Record Office has a good collection of ships' logs and other related records which detail the ownership of ships, and masters' names. One of these is the log of the East India Company Ships dating from 1668 to 1707 in a collection of estate and family papers which include details of journeys to Madras, the Bay of Bengal and St Helena. Others to be found are a collection of harbour masters' log books, a journal of John Heath Pearson concerning the voyage of the *Rutlandshire* to Calcutta in the 1860s and tradesmen's bills for equipping ships.

Norfolk Record Office also has a good collection of ships' logs and registers of ships from local ports, such as the Registry of Seamen and Shipping, 1825–

1994. An example of other related records held there are ships' papers for the period 1818 to 1895 amongst the papers of the Press family of Great Yarmouth who were merchant mariners. These include log books, wages accounts, certificates of character and discharge, a certificate of freedom from plague in 1857 and expenses.

The Suffolk offices also have a wide collection of local records relating to ships, shipping and trade along the coast, including port records for Ipswich.

Port Books are customs' accounts, inaugurated in 1565 in an attempt to increase royal revenue by more efficient collection of duties. They continued to 1799, when they were discontinued as unreliable. Despite large levels of evasion and smuggling these can be a starting point for investigating who was involved in various trades, where they went and what goods they carried. They are kept at The National Archives, although some copies and transcripts can be found locally, such as the transcript of the Blakeney Port Books, 1567–1780 in the Kenneth Allen collection at Norfolk Record Office. A study of the King's Lynn Port Books 1610–1614, edited by Alan Metters will be published in September 2009 by the Norfolk Record Society.

Relevant references can also be found in other records. The borough records for King's Lynn for instance, include early workhouse records for King's Lynn that record payments made to the families of 'imprest' sailors in 1755 and 1763. 'Adcock's wife' for example, received a payment of two shillings and six pence on 13 March 1755 for 'laying in', then weekly payments of one shilling and six pence for several months afterwards.

3.6 Bringing it to Life

Maps such as the Chart of the Orwell and Stour River held at Ipswich Record Office which was first made in 1845 with amendments made in 1923, provide a physical image of the landscape a river passed through.

The oral histories collected by local archives include many accounts of life on the coast and waterways. The Suffolk Voices collection, as already mentioned, includes the reminiscences of Lowestoft people involved in the fishing trade.

In the 1930s letters dating from 1789 to 1783 relating to trading along the River Cam were found in the Merchant's House in Swaffham Bulbeck, Cambridgeshire. An interesting article based on a talk about this trade which was given to the Cambridgeshire Family History Society can be found on the society's webpage.

Punting on the River Cam.

River trips can be taken from the yacht harbour in Wisbech. Alternatively, punt on the River Cam in the traditional flat-bottomed boats once widely used in the Fens. Many traditional narrow boats, originally used both as homes and for transporting goods, are now used for leisure and as residences, and can be seen moored at Cambridge, Ely and elsewhere.

Brightlingsea Museum has a collection of exhibits relating to the town's maritime connections and the oyster industry.

The award winning Time and Tide Museum of Great Yarmouth Life explains the town's fishing and maritime heritage.

The Town House Museum of Lynn Life houses historical displays including what is often inaccurately claimed to be King John's Cup, part of the treasure lost by the King when his baggage train sank in the Wash in 1215.

True's Yard Fishing Heritage Museum is based in the remains of King's Lynn's fishing community, the North End, which existed for hundreds of years until demolished between the 1930s and 1960s. As well as exhibits the museum has a local history library and collection archives with family and local history resources relating to the King's Lynn area.

Sheringham Museum celebrates its long lifeboat and fishing tradition with displays of lifeboat models, original boat building tools dating back to the 1880s and information on the fishing industry.

The Museum of the Broads based in a range of traditional buildings in Stalham, associated with the wherry trade, tells the story of the history, culture and environment of the Broads.

The study centre at How Hill on the River Ant close to Ludham is housed in an impressive thatched Arts & Crafts house. The estate includes Toad Hole Cottage Museum, which gives a fascinating insight into Victorian life on the Broads.

Hilgay churchyard in Norfolk has a monument to George William Manby, who invented a rocket powered life-line that could be fired to ships in distress, His gravestone is carved with a ship, an anchor, a description of his rocket device and an inscription that ends, 'The public should have paid this tribute'.

The Henry Blogg lifeboat museum in Cromer in Norfolk tells the story of the lifeboat service, including Henry Blogg, coxswain of the Cromer lifeboat from 1910 to 1947, who became the most decorated lifeboat man in the country.

Scotch lasses at work during herring season in Great Yarmouth in 1911.

A surviving example of a 'Norfolk and Suffolk' lifeboat is the *Alfred Corry*, dedicated in 1893 and in service until 1918. She is now restored and on show at the Alfred Corry museum at Southwold Harbour. The Sailor's Reading Room museum is dedicated to the town's history, with a strong focus on fishing.

Lowestoft and East Suffolk Maritime Museum features model boats, fishing equipment in a flint built fisherman's cottage.

Halvergate Island is a coastal lagoon type reserve in the River Ore below Orford. Now a RSPB reserve, cattle were still brought to the island for summer grazing up to the 1930s.

Orford has many traditional fishermen's cottages surviving on the streets close to the quay.

3.7 Wool and Textiles Trade

Although the early history of the wool and textile industry and associated cloth exports in the region is obscure, a thriving market for wool can be inferred from the copious lists of sheep flocks in the Domesday Survey of 1086. These include flocks as large as 2,100 in West Walton in Norfolk and 1,300 in Southminster in Essex.

From at least the early Middle Ages England was famous for the quality of its wool, exporting mainly to Flanders, where the wool was woven into cloth and re-imported. Most exports were a heavy broadcloth and Colchester in Essex was one of the four towns singled out in 1250 for their specialized russet manufacture.

Despite competition from the Flemish cloth trade, East Anglia remained at the heart of an international trade in wool and textiles. Exports of raw wool increased because of England's position as a provider of fine wool, with sheep farming developing as big business. Major changes and developments occurred with the immigration of Flemish and French Protestant refugees, most notably the Walloons and Huguenots. The first migration occurred during the latter half of the sixteenth century and the second during the final decades of the seventeenth century. The latter was one of the most important movements of skilled workers and professionals out of mainland Europe, due to religious persecution, as their silversmiths, printers and weavers brought new skills and techniques to the region, particularly in the manufacture of silk, velvet and linen.

Despite competition and setbacks, the wool and textiles trade in East Anglia generally flourished until the late eighteenth and early nineteenth centuries. The contraction of trade due to wars, and the spread of new methods in the emerging industrialized centres of the North and Midlands triggered its final decline.

Many social reformers were associated with the textiles trade. Among these was Sir Thomas Fowell Buxton of Earls Colne, who was descended from a family of Coggeshall clothiers. From 1818 to 1837 he served as an MP for Weymouth, and with his friend, William Wilberforce, worked for the abolition of slavery in British dominions, achieved in 1833. He was an advocate of penal reform, visiting prisons with his Norfolk born sister-in-law, Elizabeth Fry.

3.7.1 Cambridgeshire

Although Cambridgeshire was noted for its worsted cloths, wool and textiles in the fourteenth century, its trade was never as dominant as the other three East Anglian counties. Nevertheless, wool and leather were still among the chief items being sold at the fairs of the eighteenth century. Parson Drove near Wisbech was a centre of the woad industry for many centuries. This was a plant from which a blue dye was obtained, with the last remaining woad mill only demolished in the early 1900s. It was also famously referred to in an unflattering manner as a 'heathen place' by Samuel Pepys when he stayed there in September 1663 and had to sleep in a 'sad, cold nasty chamber'.

3.7.2 Essex

Many towns and villages in Essex thrived due to the wool trade up to at least the early Middle Ages, with ports such as Brightlingsea exporting cloth to the Netherlands from as far as the west of England. From then on, the picture was more complex. Although several areas experienced a decline, Colchester's trade, for instance, was revitalized in the sixteenth century once Dutch refugees settled in the town, bringing with them techniques for producing lighter and cheaper cloth.

The general political and economic upheavals of the late seventeenth century triggered a slump in the remaining Essex wool industry. The final collapse in the eighteenth and nineteenth centuries was brought about by the Napoleonic wars which cut off Essex from its markets in Spain and Portugal. This can be seen in Witham where only two firms were still producing cloth by 1750. By the 1760s only one family, the Darbys, were still employing Witham weavers.

Some of the north Essex towns did adapt by moving into different areas of textile work or adapting new techniques. One of these was Coggeshall, which originally found fame for the white cloth it produced from the fifteenth to the mid-eighteenth centuries. Coggeshall replaced wool with silk and velvet production. Over half the population were employed in the industry in the early 1800s, but once duties on imported silk goods were lifted, Coggeshall's economy was crushed. The town managed to revive its fortunes again through developing a form of lace-making called *Tambour Lace*, introduced to the town in 1812. Production continued until after the Second World War, and the 1851 census shows Coggeshall to be one of the most industrialized places in Essex at that time.

Other wool towns such as Braintree, Bocking and Halstead retained a steady prosperity. This was partially because the manufacturing of woollen cloth was replaced by silk, then by rayon and other artificial fabrics, with Halstead the home of three large silk and crepe factories belonging to Courtauld and Co. in the nineteenth century.

3.7.3 Norfolk

The textile industry was of crucial importance to Norfolk for more than 800 years, with many of the county's churches and important buildings endowed and built by wool and textile merchants. Norfolk weavers had developed a lightweight cloth called worsted by the late thirteenth century, which took its name from the village of Worstead. This was in great demand throughout England and abroad. As time went on, other types of weaving also flourished. The eighteenth century historian Francis Blomefield describes how the late 1330s saw a great increase in Flemish stuffs, or worsted manufacture in the county, probably due to an Act passed by Edward III which promised privileges to all cloth makers of 'strange lands'.

By the sixteenth century Norwich was producing light cloths known as Norwich Stuffs, which were used for dressmaking and as furnishing fabrics. Much of the county's success as a centre for textile production was due to the influx of 'strangers'; the Dutch, French and Walloon settlers. By 1571, the 'strangers' in Norwich numbered 3,925 and textiles were exported across Europe and to India, China, the West Indies, Mexico and the Americas.

Based on the number of looms listed in the city, Daniel Defoe estimated there were 120,000 people employed in manufacturing wool and silk in

Norwich alone when he visited in 1722. Although the weaving trade had suffered a temporary decline a few years before, due to the rising popularity of painted calicoes, an Act of Parliament that prohibited the use and wearing of calicoes had promoted the wool trades revival.

The increasing shift in manufacturing textiles towards the north of England is illustrated in contemporary accounts such as the editorial in the *Norfolk Chronicle* in February 1822, which remarked that:

> We understand that the manufactory of bombazines and crepes in Norwich is likely to be affected from the circumstances of those articles being now made in considerable quantities in various parts of Lancashire at a much lower rate of wages for the weaving than that which is paid here.

Data supplied by the *Census Area Monitors* website informs us that when the census was taken in 1831 'the manufacture of bombazines out of Norwich had recovered from the depression it had endured for a long time, of which the year 1811 was deemed the mid-point'. Nevertheless, the wool and textiles industries never completely recovered, and had all but disappeared by the end of the century.

3.7.4 Suffolk

The wool trade in Suffolk also benefited from the encouragement given to developing the wool trade by King Edward III in the fourteenth century, although it too had more or less died out by the late nineteenth century. The trade here mainly consisted of the combing and spinning of wool, and the manufacture of mixed woollen and silk fabrics in places such as Gainsford, Clare and Cavendish with stays made at Ipswich and hemp drablets and fustians at Haverhill. Although perhaps better known now as the birthplace of the portrait and landscape painter, Thomas Gainsborough, Sudbury was one of the most important wool centres in the region, and features in the *Pickwick Papers* by Charles Dickens as 'Eatanswill'.

This shift in work patterns in the county can be seen in records relating to the Walesby family of Bungay. In the 1830s, Samuel Walesby is recorded as a tailor but, although some of his children remained in the trade, later generations of the family left the clothing trade to become sadlers and harness makers.

Water Street, Lavenham.

Lavenham in Suffolk, a few miles north-east of Sudbury is widely regarded as England's finest medieval town, with more than 300 historically important buildings, most built between 1400 and 1500. Its prosperity as one of the richest towns in Britain during the Middle Ages was firmly grounded in wool and textiles. In 1524 the town had thirty-three cloth making businesses and its famous blue broadcloth was exported as far as Turkey.

When the church was rebuilt in the fifteenth century to celebrate the Tudor victory at Bosworth Field it was financed through the contributions of several rich clothiers and the local Lord of the Manor, John de Vere. Early in the seventeenth century the inhabitants of Lavenham began to specialize in woolcombing and spinning, forming the backbone of the local economy for the next 200 years, before gradually dying out.

In the early years of the nineteenth century Lavenham saw large numbers of local people migrating to other parts of the country in search of work. Nevertheless, remaining local workers were able to use their traditional skills into the twentieth century in the horsehair factories making furnishings, and by making mats and matting from coconut fibre imported from India and Ceylon. However, changes in manufacturing processes resulted in the closure of all cloth factories by 1930, ending an industry which had lasted over 600 years.

3.8 Finding out More

There are many general records which can provide details on people involved with the wool and textiles trade. A forthcoming publication entitled *Tracing Your Textile Ancestors* by Vivien Teasdale (Pen & Sword Family History, March 2009) will outline the broad range of records which can be used to find out more.

Local record offices and studies libraries have a variety of relevant resources. The freemen's records for Ipswich, for instance, include details of numerous people involved in the wool and textiles trade. Other official records such as the coroners' inquests also contain many references. One such was the 1715 inquest in Norwich on 12 year old George Bird who drowned while 'washing some silk for his father at the staithe belonging to the Dyeing Office in the use of John Bird'.

Much information can be found in parish registers beyond basic baptismal, marriage and burial entries. The Burials in Woollen Act passed in 1678 to protect the wool trade meant everyone had to be buried in woollen cloth, or a fine be paid. As a result, until its repeal in 1814, burial entries often include details of affidavits made to the clerk confirming this had occurred, sometimes with the name of the person making the affidavit.

Although most records for the Walloons and Huguenots are not held locally, some copies of parish registers and other material such as letters and property records can be found (see also the chapter on Religion). Among the records of the French Walloon church in Norwich, for example, are copies of the 1565 Letters Patent allowing the Norwich Corporation to admit thirty Dutch families to 'inhabit and trade in the City and to make bays, arras, sayes, tapestry, mochadees, staments and carsey'. A copy of a comprehensive history of the Walloons called *The Walloons and their church at Norwich* by W J C Moens (Huguenot Society, 1887–8), can be found in the record office and the heritage centre.

The Huguenot Society has also published transcripts of all church registers and many other related records (see Resource Directory). Some copies can be found in local record offices, libraries and family history societies.

3.9 Bringing it to Life

In Cambridgeshire, the Parson Drove Visitors Centre includes photographs and documents tracing the village history, including woad production.

In Essex, the Braintree Working Silk Museum is housed in a former silk mill originally owned by the Courtauld family, then by Warners. It houses displays on the story of the silk industry and the Warner Textile Archive, a unique worldwide record of textile manufacture and design since the eighteenth century. Included is an extensive collection of original artwork by leading designers and major artists commissioned to produce fabric designs for palaces, stately homes, liners and hotels as well as ordinary homes.

The Saffron Walden Museum has exhibits on the saffron and wool trades, whilst one of the galleries in Braintree District Museum tells the story of the wool trade in north Essex.

Bradford Street in Bocking physically encapsulates the town's historical connections with wool. Many of its sixty-five timber-framed buildings were

Dragon Hall on King Street in Norwich, a fifteenth century merchant's trading hall.

the homes of cloth merchants and date from at least the fifteenth to the early nineteenth centuries.

Coggeshall is well worth a visit to view the numerous buildings associated with the wool and textiles trade. Amongst these is Paycoke's, a late Gothic merchant's house which has a display of the renowned local lace. The heritage centre has, amongst its exhibits, a working wool loom.

Buildings such as the Guildhall in Kings Lynn and Strangers Hall in Norwich are physical reminders of the importance of the wool and textiles trade in Norfolk. Dragon Hall in Norwich, for instance, was built for wealthy merchant, Robert Toppes in the mid-fifteenth century and is a rare and magnificent example of a medieval merchant's trading hall.

Strangers Hall Museum is a former merchant's house in Norwich with many displays on trade in the area, including clothes and textiles.

Carrow House, formerly the home of the Colman family, houses a costume and textile collection dating from the eighteenth century to the present. Open by appointment only.

St James' Mill is a Grade I listed former steam-powered yarn mill dating from 1836. It was established on the site originally occupied by the White Friars in the thirteenth century, when Samuel Bignold, founder of Norwich Insurance Company, formed a stock company to give work to unemployed spinners. After the industry collapsed it became a printing warehouse, factory and offices. Although not generally open to the public it does have occasional open days.

In Suffolk, the village of Lavenham has numerous places associated with the wool and textiles trade, all meriting a closer look. Significant are the Guildhall, which is now owned by The National Trust and houses an exhibition of 700 years of the wool trade. Others are the Little Hall, a late fourteenth century clothier's house which is now the home of the Suffolk Preservation Society.

Hadleigh was the third wealthiest town in the county in 1568 due to the cloth trade. Its impressive Guildhall dates from 1430. Many of the old houses in the market town of Clare, once a centre for the wool trade in south Suffolk are famous for their pargetting.

3.10 Other Industries

East Anglia supported other significant industries. Space does not allow elaboration of them all, but some do deserve a mention as having either had a dominant role in the region's economy, or a distinctive local feature.

The old Sun Inn at Saffron Walden in 1905 featuring decorative pargetting.

DISCOVER MORE ABOUT MILITARY HISTORY

Pen & Sword Books have over 1500 titles in print covering all aspects of military history on land, sea and air. If you would like to receive more information and special offers on your preferred interests from time to time along with our standard catalogue, please complete your areas of interest below and return this card (no stamp required in the UK). Alternatively, register online at www.pen-and-sword.co.uk. Thank you.

PLEASE NOTE: We do not sell data information to any third party companies

Mr/Mrs/Ms/Other.................Name...................................

Address..

....Postcode...................

Email address..

if you wish to receive our email newsletter, please tick here ❑

PLEASE SELECT YOUR AREAS OF INTEREST

Ancient History ❑	Medieval History ❑	English Civil War ❑
Napoleonic ❑	Pre World War One ❑	World War One ❑
World War Two ❑	Post World War Two ❑	Falklands ❑
Aviation ❑	Maritime ❑	Battlefield Guides ❑
Regimental History ❑	Military Reference ❑	Military Biography ❑

Website: www.pen-and-sword.co.uk • Email: enquiries@pen-and-sword.co.uk
Telephone: 01226 734555 • Fax: 01226 734438

Pen & Sword Books

FREEPOST SF5

47 Church Street

BARNSLEY

South Yorkshire

S70 2BR

In the second half of the nineteenth century Cambridgeshire became a centre for supplying coprolites for the fertilizer industry. These were nuggets of phosphate which many people at the time thought were the droppings of wild beasts or even extinct species. The village of Barrington was at the heart of this industry which employed thousands of men women and children until the 1930s when richer sources of coprolites were found elsewhere. Its legacy remains in the surviving agrochemical industry in the area.

Newmarket Heath has famous for its horseracing connections since the time of James I. The 1871 census, for instance, lists 1,490 people as 'horse-keeper, groom or jockey' in the county with the enumerators report commenting that there were a large number of French trainers and staff in Newmarket owing to the Franco-German war.

A large number of breweries have existed across the region for centuries. In Cambridgeshire, hops are recorded as being one of the chief items of sale at the Stourbridge fair in the eighteenth century. Essex malt was widely sold to local breweries, private customers and, from the 1750s onwards, to London, using local rivers for transport. In *Essex at Work, 1700–1815* by A F J Brown, the author uses quarters as a means of measuring how much malt was sold and describes Stansted Mountfitchet as producing 3,663 quarters in 1754 alone. Great Dunmow in Essex had seventeen public houses and two breweries. Until its closure in the 1940s malt was still made for the Dunmow Brewery by the traditional method of turning barley by hand.

In Suffolk, villages like Woodbridge and Stowmarket were well known for their malt and some long standing companies such as Adnams and Greene King still operate today. Tolly Cobbold, which took its name from the merger of two family brewers – the Tollemarches and Cobbolds – in 1957, was another long established firm, having its origins in a brewery founded in Harwich in 1723. Although the last of their breweries closed in 2002, the Greene King Brewery at Bury St Edmunds now has the rights to the name, so the old Tolly Cobbold brands still appear from time to time.

The risks and dangers in such work are revealed in the inquest of 25 year old Nicholas Bolt in 1712. He died while working in the brew house of Mr Samuel Freemoult of St George Colegate in Norwich: 'pumpering' the worte out of one door into another, he overworked the pumps, it slipped and caused him to fall in the wort'.

Although trades such as building and engineering are not unique to this region some distinctive forms of building techniques can also be found locally, with the large timber framing found on buildings in Suffolk, Essex and parts of south Norfolk only possible because of the availability of large trees. Until clay tiles first came into general use in the fourteenth and fifteenth centuries, thatching was the normal form of roofing for most buildings including public buildings and churches. Three main sources for thatch were cornfields, reed and sedge beds, with the village of Dilham reputedly having the highest number of thatched cottages in Suffolk.

Before the spread of cement in building works, chalk was extracted for brick-making, building and lime burning. Remains of old workings such as those in Bury St Edmunds, Suffolk and Grays Thurrock in Essex can be found across the region. To this day Norwich is riddled with underground workings. House and road collapses have long been recorded, with several well known events in living memory.

Lime, used for fertilizer, for mortar or as whitewash, was an important part of the region's rural economy, especially in the chalky areas of Norfolk and Suffolk as it is obtained by heating chalk to a very high temperature in a kiln. The area around Horstead and Coltishall near the Broads was renowned for having chalk of a particularly high quality. Norwich City coroners' records reveal the ever present danger involved in this work as cave collapses were common. Amongst the many cases are those of 52 year old labourer, Thomas Leavis, and his companions in 1741 at a marl pit outside St Martin at Oak Gates. The following year saw the deaths of 72 year old John Beest and another man while he was digging for chalk near the lime kiln outside Pockthorpe Gates.

Grimes Graves on the edge of Thetford Forest was one of the earliest industrial sites in England, as miners in the Neolithic period, about 4,000 years ago, dug through chalk to get at the band of flint running across this area. The village of Brandon about three miles from Grimes Graves perpetuated this industry when a government factory was established there in 1686 to meet the need for flints used in the English flintlock gun (invented in the seventeenth century). In the nineteenth century flint knappers were paid on a piece work basis, the standard rate being one shilling per thousand gunflints. They worked from 7 a.m. to 9 p.m. and a master knapper could produce 3,000 gunflints a day. In 1813 the Brandon knappers were required to supply a monthly quota of over a million musket flints.

After the Army stopped using flintlocks, production of gunflints still continued for export to America and west Africa until the late twentieth century. The Brandon knappers developed a sideline industry in the 1890s and early 1900s making replicas of prehistoric flint tools and souvenirs, and the last knapper only retired in the 1980s.

Until the development of modern day transport systems most bricks were made as close to their point of use as possible, as transporting bricks, even short distances, could dramatically increase their costs. This meant that many villages had their own brickworks, with some of the earliest recorded in north Norfolk. Several 180 foot brick chimneys still stand in Whittlesey in Cambridgeshire as a reminder of what was a local speciality.

In the sixteenth century willow baskets were made extensively in the Fenlands of Cambridgeshire, whilst paper was being manufactured near Stourbridge by the 1700s. Today, Cambridgeshire is at the forefront of technology, with Milton's Science Park the home to a number of chemical, pharmaceutical, biotechnology and biomedicine companies.

Colchester in Essex was renowned for its clock making, whilst the Royal Gunpowder Mills at Waltham Abbey was the home to explosive and gunpowder production for over 300 years from the 1600s. Data collected from census returns shows that in 1831 around thirty men were noted as employed there. Parishes in the Chigwell district such as Romford, East Ham and Woodford were also noted as having seen a significant population increase by 1861 due to increased employment at Victoria Docks and new manufacturing industries such as telegraph wire and gas. The number of people employed as carpenters and joiners in Essex also increased, reflecting the additional need for accommodation and furniture as the number of households grew. The number of boot and shoemakers, and tailors also grew during the late Victorian period and were still significant occupations at late as 1931.

The development of Stansted Airport just outside Stansted village has probably had the biggest impact on the physical landscape of this area. This was established in 1942 as a United States Air Force base. In 1966 this came under control of the British Airports Authority. Since then the airport has grown significantly, providing undoubted economic and occupational benefits to the local area. Nevertheless, many local people have concerns about its impact on the local physical environment.

In Norfolk by the eighteenth century two other large industries emerged: tanning and leatherwork, leading to shoemaking, and malting and brewing. Shoemaking thrived until the mid-twentieth century, when, like so many other manufacturing industries it suffered from overseas competition. Norwich was the centre of this trade and became the home of international companies such Clarkes and Start-rite, and producing Army boots for the British Army and its Allies during the First World War. Shoes are still made in the city today.

Another important business employing thousands of people was chocolate, first through the founding of Caley's in 1883. This became part of Mackintosh, then the Rowntree group and finally Nestlé. The first impression of many visitors to the city until the factory closed in 1994 was the all pervading and inescapable smell which wafted across Norwich from the city centre factory. For many incomers like me this was probably the moment we fell in love with the city. Chocolate still features as an industry in Fakenham, and the Caley's name was revived some years ago as a cottage industry.

In Suffolk other trades and industries include the making of sacking at Stowmarket and bricks and tiles at a number of places. In the heart of the county lies Debenham which once had a flourishing rush-weaving industry.

3.11 Finding out More

Information on people who worked in these industries and trades appear in many records already mentioned. Again though, by looking at a wider range of records associated with work, trade and business it is possible to find all kinds of hidden gems.

This is illustrated by the 1839–42 marriage settlement and related papers of Emily Fisher and Robert Seaman. These form part of the King Street Brewery records and reveal that a marriage contract was drawn up to protect Emily's inheritance which included several pubs. Following her death, her husband sold them to the brewery and these documents remained with the deeds as they formed part of the record of ownership.

The Brewery History website promotes research into all aspects of the brewing trade. This includes lists of defunct breweries and descriptions of their liveries for all four counties at www.breweryhistory.com

Nationwide lists of business records can be found on the National Register of Archives www.nationalarchives.gov.uk/nra

Although many company records for businesses such as Rowntree-Mackintosh, which became part of much larger conglomerates, are held at either the headquarters of the parent company or in the archives where they are based, it is still possible to find such material locally.

Businesses frequently have staff service and pension records such as work magazines featuring the achievements of staff, those who have gone to war or retired, press cuttings relating to the business and employees or attendance books.

Ordnance survey maps show the distribution of mine workings and many are mentioned in trade directories. Details appear in official records, most of which are kept at The National Archives. Some of these are the annual reports under the 'Metalliferous Mines Regulation Act' compiled by government inspectors, which record the location of mines and type of minerals worked. The Peak District Mines Historical Society has a list for 1896 on their website www.pdmhs.com The list for Suffolk includes the names and addresses of the local agent and owners of mines on Ling Heath in Brandon and records the minerals worked as flint and chalk.

Once more, local newspapers carry countless articles and advertisements relating to trade and business of all kinds.

Colman's Archives include both the records relating to their own business as well as a phenomenal collection of general local history material of interest to the family historian. Whilst some of their business records are kept in the archives of parent company Unilever, there is still much to be found at the Norfolk Record Office and Heritage Centre. Helen Caroline Colman, daughter of Jeremiah James, published a memoir of the family in 1905 (Chiswick Press) which includes many details about the history of the company as well as photographs. Copies can be found at the heritage centre. Records held by Unilever can only be accessed by appointment through Unilever plc, Unilever Archives & Records Management, PO BOX 69, Port Sunlight, Wirral CH62 4ZD. Tel: 0151 6414551. Email: archives@unilever.com

There are many websites devoted to the history of local pubs. Among these indexes to Essex and Suffolk public houses, inns and taverns can be found at *The Historical Directory for Pubs in the South East of England* at http://londonpublichouse.com A list for Norfolk can be found at: www.norfolkpubs.co.uk/index.htm

3.12 Bringing it to Life

Many of the 'other industries' featured have displays and exhibitions in the regions museums and heritage centres.

The Museum of Technology, housed in a Victorian sewage pumping station in Cambridge features many examples of local industrial technology.

The Whittlesey Museum, Cambridgeshire, features many displays including brick making, a blacksmith's forge and wheelwright's bench.

The limekiln at Coltishall can be accessed via the adjacent Railway Tavern in Station Road. Access may be restricted between October and March due to hibernating bats.

Another surviving lime kiln can be found on private land near the Limeburners public house in Offton in Suffolk. Photographs of the kiln at various points in its history are displayed in the pub and on their website www.limeburners.co.uk/pub_history.htm

Great Dunmow Museum, Essex, is based in a rare surviving example of a small timber-framed maltings and has exhibitions about the area's social history and economic development.

Colchester's position as a centre of clock making between 1640 and 1860 is featured in Tymperleys Clock Museum.

The Royal Gunpowder Mills at Waltham Abbey provides a fascinating glimpse into the history of this work.

Coggeshall Grange Barn, dating from around the thirteenth century, is an example of local building techniques, and one of the oldest surviving timber-framed building in Europe,

The former gasworks in Fakenham, Norfolk, have been turned into a Museum of Gas and Local History.

The Bridewell Museum in Norwich was originally a prison for women and beggars, but is now dedicated to preserving the history of Norfolk's crafts and industries. The displays feature objects and machinery demonstrating how people earned their living, including shoe making and a seventeenth century Jacquard loom.

Colmans opened the Mustard Shop in Norwich in 1973 to commemorate the 150th anniversary of Jeremiah Colman taking his nephew James into partnership. It features displays of vintage containers and advertisements.

Norwich Guildhall houses a tea room and displays of memorabilia relating to the Caley's chocolate works.

Brandon Heritage Centre tells the story of the flint knapping industry in this area.

Chapter Four

CONFLICT

From William the Conqueror to the present day, East Anglian people have bred political and religious dissent, supported rural revolts and been affected by all national and international conflicts.

East Anglia was the centre for one of the greatest social revolutions in medieval England when the economic consequences of the Black Death and the introduction of the Poll Tax triggered the Peasants' Revolt of 1381. This began in response to frequent war taxes, but grew into a protest against the state of English society in general. Protesters poured into London from Kent and Essex and the protest lasted a fortnight, spreading across the south and east of England. When it was finally suppressed, more than 500 rebels had been killed and the leaders executed.

Further revolts took place in the sixteenth century when unrest over inflation, price rises, food shortages and the enclosure of land led to a series of uprisings. As the wool and cloth trades prospered landowners profited more from sheep and pasture than tillage, and embarked on large-scale enclosure of common land traditionally shared by villagers for grazing their livestock. Enclosure riots swept the country. The most serious of these was Kett's rebellion in Norfolk which lasted for six weeks between July and August 1549.

Local protests began in Wymondham when landowner Robert Kett led commoners to Norwich in protest. This ultimately led to more than 20,000 rebels challenging local and central authorities. For those who took part the penalties could be severe as in the account by Walter Rye of four tenants of the manor of Burnham Thorpe; Edward Comber, John Water, Robert Palmer and Walter Buckham, who forfeited all their lands for 'collecting together at Rysing Chase and Mussold Heath with Wm Kett'. Thousands were killed before Kett's forces were defeated. Robert Kett was hanged from the walls of Norwich Castle as a 'felonious and malicious traitor' and his body suspended on a gibbet for many months. His brother William was hanged from the west tower of Wymondham Abbey. A plaque commemorating the rebellion can be seen on the outside of Norwich Castle.

During the Civil War of 1642–1660 East Anglia was generally supportive of the Commonwealth. Cambridge became the headquarters of Cromwell's Eastern Counties Association in 1643. In Essex the administration of the county's affairs remained firmly under the control of a group of Puritan gentlemen, notably Sir Thomas Barrington. Colchester came under siege in 1648 when a Royalist Army was attacked by Parliamentarians and forced to retreat into the town, where they resisted for eleven weeks before surrendering.

King's Lynn was the main Royalist exception in Norfolk, which resulted in it being besieged and captured by the Parliamentarians in 1643. Miles Corbett of Great Yarmouth is evidence of the county's strong Parliamentarian sympathies. He was Cromwell's lawyer and signed the death warrant of Charles I. After the restoration of monarchy he was hanged, drawn and quartered at Tyburn in 1662.

Parish registers and records often reveal how the conflict affected parish affairs as when Hammond Craske was listed in the records of St John Maddermarket in 1644:

> A list of the names of all persons above the age of sixteene yeares, with a particuler of such armes as are in the custodie of such person over and above the armes perteininge to the Trained Bande … and hath one Muskett & a halbird.

Craske's burial in the same parish in 1650 refers to him as a 'strong Parliamentarian' illustrating how registers may even include the political sympathies of the incumbent and parishioners. Parish registers for Honing in Norfolk on the other hand, provide a glimpse into the trials of local people who supported the Royalists. In 1653 it records the baptisms of four children of William and Elizabeth Chamber in Lichfield in Staffordshire, with a note that William 'withdrew from his estate on account of his adherence to Charles 1st'.

The seventeenth century saw fighting with the Dutch at sea, off Lowestoft and Southwold in Suffolk, in wars over trade and overseas expansion, with a major naval battle taking place in 1672 at Sole (Southwold) bay when the combined fleets of France and England engaged in battle with the Dutch.

Southwold's Gun Hill takes its name from the six cannons, believed to be sixteenth century, and mounted there pointing out to sea. During the First World War the guns were mistaken for fortifications, resulting in Southwold being bombarded by the Germans. The guns were removed and buried, then returned to Gun Hill in the 1920s. They were buried again in the Second World War, before once again being returned in peacetime.

Landguard Fort near Felixstowe in Suffolk dates from Tudor times and remained an important stronghold until the end of the Second World War, successfully deterring an attempted Dutch raid on Harwich in 1667 during the Anglo-Dutch Wars. Amongst the Lieutenant Governors based there was Philip Thicknesse who directed in his will that his hand should be cut off and sent to his estranged son; whilst another, Robert Gosnold, made the six ringleaders of a mutiny at the fort draw lots as to which one should be condemned to death.

During what became known at the Seven Years War in the middle of the eighteenth century, men were mobilized under landowners such as George Townshend of Raynham in Norfolk who, in 1757, steered the Militia Bill through Parliament, founding a nationwide force of volunteers.

Felixstowe ferry in the 1920s with the Martello tower in the background.

During the Napoleonic Wars, when French invasion was a real possibility, a series of Martello Towers was constructed by Royal Engineers between 1805 and 1812. Eighteen were built along the Suffolk coast from Aldeburgh to the Orwell Estuary, with others in Essex, at Walton and Clacton. Based on the design of the tower on Cape Mortella in Corsica they were built as circular gun-emplacements with extremely thick walls and formed the first link in a chain of warning signals whereby fires were lit on high points, usually the church tower. The last tower was completed in 1812, the same year Napoleon was driven back from the Russian front, negating the threat of invasion, and leaving the newly built towers one of the most costly coastal defences in English history.

From 1802 the danger of invasion kept the country on alert until Norfolk born Admiral Lord Horatio Nelson destroyed the enemy fleets at Trafalgar in 1805. Schooled in Norwich and North Walsham, Nelson joined the Navy in 1770, rising through the ranks until he was promoted to admiral in 1801. The Norfolk diarist Parson Woodforde of Weston Longville wrote several times of celebrating his victories:

> 1798. Novbr, 29, Thursday ... Great Rejoicings at Norwich to day on Lord Nelsons late great & noble Victory over the French near Alexandria in Egypt. An Ox roasted whole in the Market-Place &c. ...I gave my servants this Evening after Supper some strong-Beer and some Punch to drink Admiral Lord Nelson's Health.

> 1801. Octbr. 21, Wednesday. .. Great Rejoicings to be to day on Account of Peace. A bullock to be roasted in the Market-Place.

Victory in the war with France produced the conditions under which imperial expansion could flourish. Inevitably, there were clashes with rivals leading to other conflicts and wars such as the Crimean and Boer Wars. During the First World War East Anglia came under attack from the sea from German battlecruisers whilst airships and bombers ranged over the region by night. Thousands of men from the region were killed fighting on land, sea and air. Amongst the many who served their country was Flora Sandes from Marlesford in Suffolk, who served in Serbia and became the first woman to hold a commission in the Serbian Army and the only woman to officially enrol as a soldier during the First World War.

One of the most famous women in the First World War was Edith Cavell, the daughter of the vicar of Swardeston in Norfolk. She was executed by the

Army encampments at Swaffham in Norfolk in 1915.

Germans in 1915 for helping British officers escape from Brussels. Her famous last words were 'I realize patriotism is not enough. I must have no hatred or bitterness towards anyone.' Originally buried at Westminster her body was transferred to Norwich Cathedral after the war and a statue to her stands outside its walls.

Also in 1915 an event occurred involving the 'Vanished Battalion' of Gallipoli: the 5th Norfolks. This became a legend when one of the companies which had been recruited from royal servants on the Sandringham estate apparently vanished into thin air during an attack on Turkish positions.

The youngest survivors of the First World War were still young enough to fight in the Second World War twenty years later and older survivors joined the Home Guard. There were several military airfields already in existence in Norfolk in 1939 and thirty more were built over the next five years. Bomber Command was joined in 1942 by the Americans of the 8th Air Force's 2nd Air Division and their airfields were spread across the south and east of the county as well as in Suffolk and Cambridgeshire.

In addition to the Air Force, Army camps proliferated and the Royal Navy also had bases off the coast. Between 1942 and 1945 3 million American military and auxiliary men and women passed through Great Britain. In 1944 for example, there were over 71,000 Americans living in Suffolk alone, with nineteen USAAF airbases constructed between 1942 and 1943 for the use of the 8th Army Air Force. Elvedon Hall was the Divisional Headquarters and Woodbridge airfield was used as an Emergency Landing Group.

The Stanford Battle Area on the edge of Thetford forest was a British Army infantry training area established in 1942. The villages of Buckenham Tofts, Langford, Stanford, Sturston, Tottington and West Tofts were cleared of inhabitants so the Army could use the area, and four churches still remain. Still in use by the Army, the area is only open for special tours a number of days a year with some specifically for former residents and their relatives.

Radar, which was used for the first time in the Second World War to detect enemy aircraft, was first developed at Bawdsey on the Suffolk coast by Sir Watson-Watts and his team. The minesweepers based at Lowestoft in the Second World War were part of the Royal Naval Patrol Service, otherwise known as 'Harry Tate's Navy'. Its headquarters was at Sparrow's Nest, the municipal pleasure ground at Lowestoft. Whilst the specially formed submarine hunting groups had fast, well-equipped ships, the anti-submarine trawlers were relatively humble and unglamorous. Both groups proved invaluable in the fight against the German U-boat fleet.

The Air Ministry formed a secret department which constructed decoy airfields and other devices along the east coast, designed to fool the German Luftwaffe. Their aim was to lure bombers away from Lowestoft and other ports with one of the first being placed at Sutton Heath in Suffolk.

Duxford in Cambridgeshire was one of the many airfields built as an RAF fighter base in 1918. It was operational once more during the Second World War, and involved in the 'Big Wing' controversy, a tactic which involved meeting incoming Luftwaffe bombing raids in strength with a wing-sized formation of three to five squadrons. Essex airbases were also famous during the Battle of Britain as Fighter Command pilots from Hornchurch, Debden, Rochford and North Weald took a leading part.

4.1 Finding out More

Although many records relating to soldiers, sailors and airmen are held at The National Archives or other national archives, there are still a large number of resources held locally in record offices, libraries and museums.

Tracing Your Army Ancestors by Simon Fowler (Pen & Sword, 2006) and *Tracing Your Air Force Ancestors* by Phil Tomaselli (Pen & Sword, 2007) both supply essential guides to all aspects of Army and Naval research.

Regimental Museums contain much useful and interesting material for finding out more about people who served with local regiments although they tend to hold much more information about officers than other ranks. Nevertheless, their displays of medals, memorabilia and photographs provide useful general historical information. Some details of individuals from these collections can be found online. For example, a search for the surname Seaman in the Norfolk Regimental Museum collection, via the NOAH website, brings up several references including a campaign medal, postcards and photographs.

Census, certificates, parish registers et al will frequently show details of people's connections to the Army and Navy, or more recently the Air Force. One example is Benjamin Naylor whose occupation was given as a Chelsea pensioner when the 1851 census was taken in Elsing. Another example from parish registers is the baptism of Eliza Thornton in Maldon All Saints and St Peter, Essex in 1814, where her father John was described as a sergeant in '83 Regiment'.

Court records can include petitions for financial assistance from retired or injured soldiers and sailors. One example among the petitions to the Essex Quarter Sessions is one in 1677 for a pension from a Barking sailor badly injured in the Dutch Wars. Another in 1678 is from an 'impressed' seaman at Colchester who lost a leg fighting in the Dutch Wars.

In Suffolk, the Lowestoft Record Office has an interesting series of Naval Log Books belonging to the Aldous family from 1729 to 1737 and 1779 to 1783, originally bequeathed to the local museum. These include details of journeys from England to Carolina and to Mederas [sic] between 1729 and 1737 as well as journals of proceedings on board a number of ships between 1779 and 1783.

The Ipswich office has a collection of correspondence spanning several centuries called 'Ipswich Borough correspondence and other miscellaneous purchases'. Among the variety of topics are several references to battles with the Dutch in the seventeenth and eighteenth centuries. These include the transfer of sick and wounded, including the Dutch commander, to Ipswich as prisoners in 1653; payments for their care and repatriation and mention of men wounded in battle being sent to Yarmouth for care in 1753.

Certain areas such as Colchester have had long standing associations with the armed forces and, once again, trade directories can be used to find out the history and whereabouts of training camps and Army, Navy and Air Force bases. For example, Essex directories in the 1870s describe Colchester as:

The depot of the 44th regiment (The Essex Regiment) and the head quarters of the 3rd Essex (Rifles) Militia and of the west Essex Militia, which formed respectively the 3rd and 4th battalions of the regiment based at Little Warley.

The Militia was a voluntary county based part-time force for home defence. It ceased to be summoned after the Civil War, but was revived in 1757, when the Militia Act established Militia Regiments in all counties of England and Wales. The Yeomanry (cavalry) and the Volunteers were introduced later. In 1808 a further force, the Local Militia, was formed. By 1816 the Local Militia and the Volunteers had been dissolved but the Volunteer Force was revived in 1859. In 1907, the Yeomanry and the Volunteers combined as the Territorial Force, and in 1908 the Militia was revived as the Special Reserve.

Each year, the parish was supposed to draw up lists of adult males, and to hold a ballot to choose those who had to serve in the militia. Where they survive these militia lists provide a census of all men between the ages of 18 and 45 from 1758 to 1831. The surviving lists, held locally, can be very informative, giving details about individual men and their family circumstances. However, the coverage is not complete. For more information see J S Gibson and Medlycott, *Militia Lists and Musters, 1757–1876* (4th ed., FFHS, 2000).

Copies of militia lists and musters can be found in all local offices. The Essex office, for example, has muster rolls and lists giving the names and other details of officers and men in the Essex militia from circa 1775 to 1865. These can be found among records of the Lord Lieutenant, borough and parish records.

Norfolk has many references to notices of assembly, costs and the appointment of officers relating to the militia amongst various collections of private papers. The Petre of Westwick collection, for example, includes a claim for training allowances for the 1st Western Militia in 1810, whilst the Chandler collection has an undated account book of Sergeant James Kemp relating to the East Norfolk Militia.

An interesting collection amongst the Beeston of Preston papers includes a 'Third Register of Norfolk Militia subdivision book' which is a register of soldiers dating from around 1799 that gives their age, appearance, trade, place of birth and parish. There are also registers of returns and standing order books dating from the 1790s which provide information on the movements of the troops, appointments and promotions.

Parish records often contain documents specifically relating to military records, especially muster notices and expenses. Poor men often enrolled in the militia as substitutes in return for payment from those eligible for service who wished to avoid it. If the wives and children of militia substitutes needed poor relief the parish could apply to the County Treasurer for reimbursement. The parish of Dersingham in Norfolk is just one which includes such records, including two demands by the county treasurer for a contribution from the parish towards maintaining the wives and children of militia men serving as substitutes. Also included is a certificate of enrolment of militia substitutes in 1804 which states that:

> Thomas Rix of Darsingham Blacksmith was on the 1st August last lawfully chosen by ballot to serve in the Army of Reserve for the said Parish ... And that on the 9th. Day of August last he produced John Simkin of Great Burnham Labourer who was lawfully approved of, sworn and to serve in the said Army according to Law as Substitute for the said Thomas Rix ... he the said Thomas Rix who was chosen by ballot as aforesaid is become intitled to our Order to receive the following Sum of Money ... Eleven Guineas (which we adjudge to be half the current Price paid for a Volunteer in the said County) out of the Rate made for and producing Volunteers.

A militiaman's discharge certificate from the same parish in 1810 states that Miles Hamerton, has served 'honestly faithfully for the space of Seven years and Three Months But in consequence of his having provided a Substitute to continue his Service is hereby discharged. This goes on to provide a description:

> He is Aged about 31 years, 5 feet 4 inches high, fair complexion, Lt Brown hair, Grey eyes, Round visage, born in the parish of Ringstead by trade a Cordwainer.

Parish records can contain an even wider variety of records with personal details of those in the armed services. One instance is a biography compiled in 1943 by the local vicar of Fritton in Norfolk which describes the life of William Goat who was awarded the Victoria Cross for his part in the Indian Mutiny of 1858. This includes William's photograph and own account. Other records which can be found include details of subscriptions paid towards war memorials by local people. A moving bundle of letters from local men at the front in the First World War, thanking parishioners for gifts of food and postal orders, survive in the Stow Bedon records.

Many contemporary accounts exist of wartime experiences from both the First and Second World Wars. An account of bombing raids by Zeppelins in May 1917 at Raynham and Knapton by J Walter Cole, the local recruiting agent for the North Walsham district, makes fascinating reading. This can be found at Norfolk Record Office in a notebook he used for recording how many men he recruited and from where. In it he states: 'Fred Pyle was killed at Wellingham, 2 horses killed at West Raynham & Mrs Hart's House wrecked by Zeppelins'. Later the same year he describes an air raid: 'Walcott Hall; church, farm, 2 Horses killed, Mrs Love struck by bombs from Zeppelin about 20 bombs fell between Lighthouse Trim & East Ruston mill'.

Company and parish magazines often ran articles about employees and local people in the armed forces.

Local newspapers include countless wartime reports. The *Ipswich Journal* in July 1849, for example, reported the death of Timothy Claxton who was 'killed at the battle of Chillianwalla, in an engagement with the Sikhs'. This described him as the second son of Mr Robert Claxton, a shoemaker of Bungay, and described his military career.

During the First World War, local papers featured many extracts of letters sent to relatives from those on active service and reports of visits home on leave as well as reports about those who signed up, often accompanied by photographs. In the early stages of the war these reports were spread throughout the papers. As the war progressed specific pages entitled 'War News' begin to appear with less local detail and longer and longer lists of casualties. The *Downham Market Gazette* for instance had a list of the names of those 'Previously reported missing, now reported prisoners of war (all Suffolk Regiment)' under the header 'LOCAL CASUALTIES' on 10 April 1915.

The survival of official surveys into bomb damage varies for each county. The majority date from the Second World War and the main types of records providing details about people and places affected are: air raid precaution files which include reports into unexploded bombs, shells and mines, bomb censuses and civil defence wardens and police reports. The lists of exploded bombs for instance record the location, type of bomb, size of crater, numbers of injured and numbers and names of those killed. One example from these are the numerous reports of unexploded bombs in the Needham Market area of Suffolk during the Second World War. Included amongst these are the

Bomb damage in 1915 to St Peter's church, Great Yarmouth.

names of many properties and owners such as Clamp Farm in Creeting St Peter occupied by John Forrest.

Maps of unexploded ordnance across the region, based on research in national and local archives, can be found on the Zetica website www.zetica.com

The online databases produced by Cambridgeshire Family History Society at www.cfhs.org.uk include: Crimean Casualties from the 30th Foot (Cambridgeshire Regiment), the 30th Foot Discharge Papers taken from records stored at The National Archives and deaths recorded on Boer War Memorials in Cambridge, Ely, Huntingdon, Bedford and Peterborough.

The GENUKI site has links to large numbers of village and local history websites include details from memorials to war dead, and many local memorials are listed on the Role of Honour website www.roll-of-honour.com The National Inventory of War Memorials database is working to compile a listing of every war memorial in the UK. www.ukniwm.org.uk

4.2 Bringing it to Life

All the Regimental Museums in the region have exhibitions on the history of local regiments and military connections.

The Imperial War Museum at Duxford, Cambridgeshire hosts an outstanding collection of over 150 historic aircraft and a reconstructed wartime operations room.

The American Cemetery in Madingley commemorates the 3,800 dead and 5,000 missing in action American service personnel who were based in Cambridgeshire.

In Essex, Colchester Castle is a museum with many hands-on displays featuring Colchester's history from the Stone Age, including its establishment as a Roman garrison and its role during the Civil War.

The village of Great Wigborough experienced a visit from a German airship, Zeppelin L33, during the First World War when it crashed in the village in 1916. A plaque commemorating the event can be found in St Stephen's church, framed by aluminium taken from the wreck.

The East Essex Aviation Society and Museum located in a Martello Tower at Point Clear contains displays of wartime aviation, military and naval photographs and memorabilia with local and US Air Force connections.

Great Massingham in Norfolk hosts an annual display of artefacts associated with the now disused airfield east of the village, which was a centre for bomber command.

The 100th Bomb Group Memorial Museum on the edge of the disused Dickleburgh airfield in Langmere includes a tribute to the US 8th Air Force which was stationed here. It includes displays of USAAF decorations and uniforms, equipment, combat records and other memorabilia.

The Millennium Library in Norwich has a roll of honour and memorial library in honour of the 2nd Air Division of the USAAF personnel, based in Norfolk and Suffolk, who were killed in the line of duty.

A poignant memorial is the military section, also known as the soldiers' plot, in the north-east corner of Earlham Cemetery in Norwich. This includes more than 200 graves and memorials from the 1870s with a centrepiece sculpture entitled 'Spirit of the Army' by Norfolk born sculptor John Bell, whose previous works had included the Crimean War Artillery Memorial at Woolwich.

Initially those buried here were peacetime soldiers based at one of the city's barracks who died as a result of accident or sickness. The majority are of soldiers from the First World War, but there are some airmen and one boy seaman, many of whom died in local hospitals and were too far away from their homes to be buried there. One especially interesting Commonwealth War Graves Commission headstone marks the grave of Captain and Quartermaster George Clements of the Royal Dragoons, and veteran of the Crimean battles of the Alma, Balaclava and Inkerman who died in 1916 age 85.

In Suffolk, the Battle of the Armada in 1588 was commemorated in Lowestoft with the erection of the Armada Post 100 years later. The post has the initials 'TM' for Thomas Meldrum, owner of the *Elizabeth*, which was used as a fire ship in the battle. The post has been renewed at 100 year periods since by the Lowestoft and East Suffolk Maritime Society.

The Parham Airfield Museum is home to the US 390th Bomb Group Memorial Air Museum and Museum of the British Resistance Organization

Bawdsey Radar Museum, Bawdsey Quay, IP12 3AZ, based in wartime concrete bunkers, is the home of the first radar station in the world

The Royal Naval Patrol Museum in Lowestoft commemorates the minesweeping service with its displays of models, photographs, documents and uniforms. Nearby is the War Memorial Museum dedicated to those who served during the Second World War.

The Harry Tate's Navy website is dedicated to the history of the Royal Naval Patrol Service and includes video clips and memoirs. www.harry-tates.org.uk

Chapter Five

CRIME

After the Conquest, the Anglo Saxon legal system was slowly replaced by the Norman system as Justices of the Peace (JPs) took over much of what had been the Sheriff's work. Quarter Sessions courts were established in 1349 and Justices of the Peace were originally required to meet four times a year at each compass point in each county on a rotation system. Serious cases like murder were tried by visiting Assize Judges from London and there was initially some overlap in cases dealt with by Manor courts.

By the late sixteenth century the foundations of our modern legal system were established and the duties of the Justices increased as government extended its regulatory control during the Tudor and early Stuart periods. During the Civil War and Interregnum, County Committees took over many legal functions in Parliamentary areas. This was mainly the collecting of taxes and administering revenue, although they did gradually acquire other powers. In Royalist districts similar procedures were adopted, but not as successfully.

As work increased for the Justices of the Peace, some devolution of work took place and magistrates, either alone or in twos or threes, were given authority to deal with a variety of offences. They met more frequently and could give cheap, quick local justice. This led to the development of Petty Sessions during the seventeenth and eighteenth centuries, the boundaries of which often coincided with the old hundreds.

The types of cases and information to be found amongst these court records include: debtors, assault, theft, trespass, profane language, victuallers licences, licences for a dissenting ministers, fraud, appeals against removal, bastardy cases and appeals, appeals against rates, lists of prisoners and coroners expenses. Two examples from Cambridgeshire, for which references can be found in the Cambridge Record Office card indexes, are: Ann Fuller who was fined one shilling plus eighteen shillings costs at the Michaelmas Session in 1860 for assault and battery on Mary Ann Easey at Soham, and Alfred Larkins who was imprisoned for seven days with hard labour at the Epiphany Sessions in 1874 for stealing a pick and shovel.

Some Norfolk examples include the Jury presentment at the Norwich Quarter Sessions in 1780 that Charles Bradfield, a farmer of Eaton, refused to take 13 year old Sarah Skipper as an apprentice, as directed by the director and acting guardians of the poor for the hundred of Forehoe. Another is the Jury presentment at the Norfolk Sessions in Swaffham in 1795 that 'the road leading from Swaffham to King's Lynn through West Bilney, lying in Pentney is obstructed by gates built across it by inhabitants of Pentney'.

The practical business of policing was mainly undertaken by the parish constable who was appointed from amongst local ratepayers to administer law enforcement within that parish. Their duties included 'watch and ward', taking care of the parish armour and supervising the local militia and alehouses. They were also responsible for the removal of paupers, apprehending wayward fathers in bastardy cases and administering punishments such as whipping vagrants.

This spread of duties is illustrated by the collection of constable records amongst the Friston parish records in Suffolk. These include accounts, orders to the constable to bring rogues before the JPs at Woodbridge and Saxmundham, further orders to return lists of those qualified to serve in the

The dungeons in the old tollhouse in Great Yarmouth in circa 1930.

Records of expenses in Quarter Sessions records for this period also reveal some of the practical problems caused when the authorities had to deal with turbulent situations. For instance, references in the Quarter Sessions papers for Huntingdonshire include a protest from the Chief Constables of the county in 1834 against a reduction in their salaries. In this they point out their exacting duties which involved travelling 500 miles and the upkeep of a horse, as well as making specific reference to their increased responsibilities during the riots which occurred in the county in 1830.

There are a variety of other local records that supply information on the background of those who came before both the Assize and Quarter Sessions courts. Among these are the indictments which record what someone was charged with, their residence and occupation. Prison registers often include personal details such as a birthplace, physical descriptions or even photographs. Prison officials kept various books and journals recording details of day to day life in a prison. Prison diaries, in particular, have entries relating to disputes, illnesses, burials, escapes, punishments, transfers, arrangements for transportation and the death sentence being carried out. Other records which may be found in local collections include registers of convictions for night poaching and lists of cases regarding legal aid applications.

Among those for Cambridgeshire and Huntingdonshire are sessions rolls and bundles from 1730, order books from 1660, recognizance registers from 1661 to 1757 (with gaps), licensed victuallers recognizance registers from 1728 to 1838 and registers of gamekeepers from 1804. The majority are held at the record office, although some very early records for Ely can be found at Cambridge University Library. The Cambridge office also holds a card index to all persons accused or convicted at Petty and Quarter Sessions between 1660 and 1883 (with gaps).

Essex has Quarter Sessions records dating from 1500 to 1971, including sessions bundles from 1670 to 1919. Their catalogues to these records include some summaries of the wide variety of cases included. For example, there is an order for the relief of vagrants with passes from Derbyshire and the petition of two Lascars, natives of Calcutta, who had been imprisoned for thirteen months because they 'got Astray in the Country' in 1787; a notice in 1762 to the Collector of Excise for an allowance on duty for malt spoilt when being shipped from Mistley Thorn to London; and a Welsh woman arrested for begging and wandering in Tillingham in 1726.

Both Cambridgeshire and Suffolk Record Offices have a series of indexes, arranged by name, to cases held in the Assize and Quarter Sessions courts.

Most of these are on card indexes, but in the case of Suffolk, there are also some printed lists. The Cambridgeshire indexes are taken from the Quarter Sessions minute books, but the Suffolk indexes come from a much wider range of sources including gaol books and calendars of prisoners.

Norfolk Quarter Sessions records date from circa 1350 to 1971. The Norfolk Record Office has draft transcripts to a large number of the sessions papers available on request

The Suffolk collection dates from circa 1309 to 1971. As mentioned above, there are some indexes to these records, including the minute books from 1639 to 1791 in card indexes and on their search room shelves.

Lists of surviving Quarter Sessions records in local record offices can also be found on the A2A website. Some of these include people's names and summary details of particular cases, as in the case of the Essex Record Office listings on their SEAX online catalogue.

Another useful and fascinating source is the Calendars of Prisoners. These are typewritten lists of every prisoner held in the gaol awaiting trial at certain dates, published as broadsheets and included in local newspapers. They include details of the crime each prisoner was charged with, where they were arrested, and occasionally, handwritten notes as to whether they were convicted or acquitted. They generally give the place and date of trial. All four counties have some filed amongst the Quarter Sessions papers, and some have been published.

A particularly good collection for Norfolk survives, listing prisoners tried at Norfolk and Norwich City Quarter Sessions and Norfolk and Norwich City Assizes, dating from the early 1800s to 1896 (with gaps). The originals are held by the Norfolk Heritage Centre, with film copies at the record office. An example of one entry of someone held for trial is that of 20 year old Elijah Balls who was held for trial at the Lent Assizes in Thetford in 1829. Written in the margin is the word 'discharg' and it states he was committed on the oath of Jonas Syer of Croxton, a labourer, and his wife Elizabeth, with having 'stolen a pair of breeches, an umbrella, and a quantity of bread and flour, from out of his dwelling-house'.

Most cases of people transported were heard by the Assize Courts and those records are kept at The National Archives. However, there are still a considerable number of records held locally.

Nearly all criminal cases, especially the most serious, were reported in local newspapers. For example, the *Norfolk Chronicle & Norwich Gazette* reported that a George Browne aged 22 was sentenced to ten years transportation at the Quarter Sessions in October 1852 for breaking into a house in Hargham and stealing three shillings and three pence from Annie Seed's purse and breaking into another home in Shropham.

Lists of convicts transported to Australia for the period 1787–1867, compiled from British Home Office records, can be found at www.slq.qld.gov.au/info/fh/convicts

An extremely useful source is the Transportation Index on the shelves at Norfolk Record Office which gives details of people transported from cases reported in the *Norfolk Chronicle* newspaper. The printed calendars to prisoners on broadsheets, referred to above, include many prisoners held in the county gaol while awaiting transportation.

Several reform schools have been set up in the region. The Red House School in Buxton in Norfolk was opened in 1853 by social reformer John Wright originally for boys or young men who had been confined in gaol in Norwich Castle. It was taken over by the Government and certified for criminals in 1855 and certified as an industrial school in 1894, before becoming the Red House Farm Approved School in 1933, and finally closing in the 1980s. During that time the school received boys from all over the country. A good set of admission and discharge registers and other records are held in Norfolk Record Office. These include progress reports made by Thomas Babington who was governor there for forty-two years from 1867 and kept records of every boy's background and progress.

In Essex, the Sir Edward's Reformatory for Roman Catholic Boys opened in 1870 at Boleyn Castle, East Ham, whilst trade directories list the Thames Reformatory School Ship *Cornwall* as lying off Purfleet. It is possible to use directories to find more about the history of this ship and others, as well as the number of boys in the school and who the captains, acting as superintendents, were.

Manor Courts dealt with a range of matters affecting the local community including enforcement of bye-laws about common land and petty crime within the manor. Although the variety of business dealt with declined steadily from the eighteenth century as their courts became increasingly focused on the administering the transfer of copyhold land, it is still possible to find references to criminal cases.

The Manorial Documents Register at The National Archives identifies the nature and location of manorial records. Much of the Register, including Norfolk, is now online at www.nationalarchives.gov.uk/mdr

Some manorial court cases have been published by local historians or historical and record societies. Walter Rye's article *Early life in the Manor of*

Burnham in *Norfolk Antiquarian Miscellany. Vol. 1*, published in 1873, illustrates the litigious nature of people in Norfolk during the medieval period by referring to a number of prosecutions recorded in the manorial court rolls for Burnham. These include trees overhanging the highway, not repairing roads, assaults, and people keeping unrung pigs, savage dogs or bulls. Other examples include a 'Robert, son of Edmund Palle, being fined sixpence under Henry VI for standing at night under the windows of John Gasele to hear his secrets', whilst the inhabitants of North Creake Abbey were frequently prosecuted for trespassing in pursuit of conies.

It is not only court records which provide details of crime and illegal activities. Many clerks made remarks in their parish registers about national and local events as when the incumbent of Pulham St Mary the Virgin made a note in the midst of the baptismal entries of 1743 about the theft of the Great Seal and Mace from the house of Lord Thurlow, Lord High Chancellor of England.

It was presumably for practical reasons that the East Tuddenham incumbent noted next to the 1723 marriage entry of Edward Barber and Mary Mallett that:

> I believe this entry to be a Forgery, made by Samuel Barber of Swanton, late of this Parish, born – Leech, in Sepr 1809 for the purpose of proving his Relationship to a Mr Barber, who died intestate at the Adelphi London, leaving a considerable fortune. Edwd Mellish. Vicar.

As was the note written next to the 1767 baptismal entry in Attlebridge for the twin sons of Mary Lincoln which stated that 'this woman was married sometime before to Thomas Lador but it appear'd upon enquiry, that the said Lador had a wife then living at Alford in Lincolnshire'.

5.3 Bringing to Life

The Old Shire Hall in Cambridge, where court cases were held, is currently the home of Cambridge Record Office.

Colchester Castle in Essex has the largest keep built in Europe. Among the many exhibitions are the dungeons where the Witchfinder General, Matthew Hopkins, interrogated locals suspected of witchcraft.

The Essex Police Museum in Chelmsford chronicles the history of the Essex police force from 1840 to the present day. As well as being a museum they collect, preserve and interpret related documentary material and have an online database listing over 3,000 officers who served between 1840 and 1930. www.essex.police.uk/museum/research.htm An associated publication called *Tales From The Essex Police Museum* has been compiled by Fred Feather for the Essex Society for Family History (Essex Family Historian Supplement, December 2007). This describes many cases and events involving local police and includes much background history.

Norwich Castle former dungeons contain displays of instruments of torture, along with death masks of some of the prisoners executed here.

The Essex Witch Trials website lists the 730 people accused of either being, or consorting with, witches. This includes details of whether or not they were tried and, if they were, what happened. www.hulford.co.uk/years.html

The Old Gaol House in King's Lynn includes sight and sound effects based around its history as a prison.

The Bridewell, or House of Correction in Bridewell Street, Wymondham was built as a model prison in 1785 along lines recommended by the prison reformer, John Howard, who had condemned the previous gaol on the site as 'one of the vilest in the country'. It has since been claimed to have been the model for penitentiaries in the United States. It is now home to several organizations including the Wymondham Heritage Museum.

Polstead is infamous for the 'Murder at the Red Barn' in the mid-nineteenth century, which subsequently inspired Gothic melodramas in print and on stage. Local girl Maria Marten was murdered by her lover William Corder and buried in the barn. Her body was discovered when her stepmother claimed to have dreamt it was there. Corder was tried and publicly hanged in Bury St Edmunds in 1848. As was the case with the bodies of many executed prisoners, his body was used as a teaching aid at West Suffolk Hospital. An original bust made of his head after his death, for the study of phrenology, and a death mask can be seen at Moyse's Hall Museum as can an account of the murder, bound in his skin.

Newspapers reports often include far more details about the background to a crime than appears in the court minute books. For instance, when the Swing Riots took place in the 1830s, local papers ran articles which were often several pages long. The Norfolk Heritage Site provides an illuminating insight into these events from a local perspective as it includes extracts from newspaper reports of events in the Reepham and Cawston area www.norfolkheritage.org.uk/reepham

Chapter Six

THE PARISH POOR

Poverty was a regular fact of life for a large number of our ancestors. It is therefore likely you will find at least one ancestor who either went through the poor law system at some point in their lives or had to pay towards maintaining the poor.

The concept of taking care of those unable to care for themselves has existed from the earliest times. By the medieval period the duty of relieving the poor was seen as the moral duty of the Church. In practice this meant the parish priest did what he could, whilst the monasteries acted as an umbrella with their infirmaries and leper houses for the sick and infirm, and extensive lands on which the able bodied could work.

One of the consequences of the suppression of the English monasteries under Henry VIII in 1536–9, and the resulting social chaos, was that this umbrella of care disappeared. Individual parishes only had voluntary contributions from locals, so were often unable to cope with the rising numbers of people turning to them for help, whilst the growing bands of wandering poor caused fear and distrust. Despite various attempts to solve it, the problem of what to do with the poor, and whose responsibility they should be, refused to go away.

The 1601 Poor Law Act formed the basis of local poor law administration for over 200 years, although it was not formally abolished until 1948. Before 1834, poor relief was the responsibility of local parish officials, who raised funds through local taxation and provided relief in the form of money, food, clothes and fuel, housing for the elderly and sick, or arranging work for the able-bodied.

Economic and agricultural depressions and a rising population led to spiralling costs in the poor relief system throughout the eighteenth and early nineteenth centuries. Although groups of parishes could save costs by joining together to set up and run their own workhouses under Gilbert's Act of 1782, this was not compulsory. Also, each parish was still responsible for maintaining their own able-bodied adult poor who remained outside the workhouse. From 1834 relieving the poor became the responsibility of groups of parishes under a union workhouse. This system remained in place until the introduction of the National Health Service as the first plank of the Welfare State in 1948.

A summary of the evolution of the poor law system from its earliest days as a parish based system, through poor law unions and up to the its formal abolition can be seen in the following key dates:

Date	Poor Laws and Acts of Parliament
1536–9	Suppression of Monasteries.
1536 Poor Law	Reinforced distinction between 'can't and won't works'. Individual parishes to care for 'impotent poor' through collection of Alms.
1547 Act	Introduced branding and slavery as punishments for persistent vagrancy.
1572	Office of overseer of the poor created.
1598 Act for Reliefe of the Poor	Overseers authorized to find work for the poor and set up parish poorhouses through local poor rates.
1601 Poor Law Act	Churchwardens and overseers appointed to maintain the poor through local taxes.
1609–1610 Poor Law Acts	Houses of Correction built. Constables appointed to search out rogues etc.
1662 Settlement Act	Everybody should have an official parish of settlement. BUT each parish responsible only for its own poor.
1691 Act	Laid down qualifications for gaining settlement in a parish.
1697 Settlement Act	Poor people could move to another parish with settlement certificate. Paupers to wear identifying badges on their shoulder.
From 1732	Parish workhouses could be set up.
1782 Gilbert's Act	Groups of parishes could set up workhouses. Repealed Act that paupers had to wear the letter 'P'.
1795	Removal of paupers could only occur after they became a charge on the rates.
1834 Poor Law Amendment Act	Replaced parish basis of poor relief and introduced Poor Law Unions with elected Boards of Guardians.
1930	Abolition of poor law guardians. Workhouses closed.
1948	Introduction of National Health Service.

6.1 Finding out More

The various attempts over time to administer to, and regulate, the poor have generated a wealth of information. The term 'poor law records' is generally used to describe one group of records amongst many other kinds of parish records. For an in-depth look at the whole range of different parish records see *The Parish Chest* by W E Tate.

These poor law records can date back to the early 1600s, and are amongst the most interesting records for family historians. Not only are they one of the few records that let us 'hear' the voices of our ancestors, they can provide us with an insight into the lives of ordinary people in a way few other documents do. Even if we do not find a record for our own ancestors, looking at others from the same area and time period can give us important insights into their lives.

Poor law records can supply information on the type of poor relief someone received, including how much they got, whether the parish bought their clothes, paid for a nurse when ill or to lay out the dead, arranged an apprenticeship for a poor child, chased an errant father for maintenance for his illegitimate child or if they lived in one of the alms houses supported by the parish or a local charity. They also list those ratepayers who had to pay the costs.

As a result you may find parish records dating back hundreds of years which tell you whether your ancestors were born in that place, who their parents were, where they worked and how much they were paid. You may also find out whether they owned or rented property of enough value to pay poor rates, if they argued about how much was due from them, and whether or not the parish had to prosecute them for non payment.

The majority of surviving parish records can be found in local record offices. Many have been referred to throughout this book already because of the insights they offer into other areas of life in the past. Probably the most informative are the churchwardens' and overseers' accounts, settlement papers and removal orders, apprenticeship records and bastardy papers. Removal orders from the parish of Winfarthing, for instance, describe how a single man called Jeremiah Revell was removed from Winfathing to Hapton in 1757 and John Ravell and his wife Lydia were removed from Bungay St Mary in Suffolk to Winfarthing in 1811. A removal order the following year, records a John Revell as a vagrant and rogue and as being removed from Beccles in Suffolk to Winfarthing.

Ray Whitehand's book *At The Overseers Door* includes information on many parish records, as it tells the story of Suffolk's parish workhouses until the introduction of the Union workhouses in 1834.

Below is a summary of the main categories and types of records that come under the general heading of poor law records, with a brief description of some of the information to be found in them.

Types of Records	Types of Information to be found
Churchwardens / Overseers accounts	Details of maintaining the poor and those who paid the poor rates.
Charity accounts	Administration of local bequests and foundations, e.g. education, dowries, food, clothing and apprenticeships.
Settlement Certificates and Examinations	Biographical and employment details and papers guaranteeing to support people moving from one parish to another.
Removal Orders	Names, occupations, marital status and ages of people being removed and where they were removed to and from.
Apprenticeship Records	Biographical and work details. Includes those arranged for paupers and through charities.
Bastardy Papers	Details of parentage and payments.
Other	Includes parish workhouses and assisted emigration.

Settlement papers refer to the documents issued when parish officials dealt with those needing to claim poor relief. In order to make decisions about whether people were entitled to financial support, the clergy and parish officers had to find out the criteria under which someone belonged to their parish. Parish officials were allowed to find out a person's place of settlement by means of a sworn statement or examination, known as a settlement examination. Relatives, past employers or other people with relevant knowledge could also be examined. If it was decided someone did not belong to a particular parish, a removal order could be issued sending a pauper back to their parish of settlement. Settlement certificates permitted people to move about by guaranteeing their own parish would receive them back, or support them financially where they were living. Certificates were sometimes issued retrospectively and do not necessarily mean that the person referred to was a pauper so they may not appear in any other poor law records.

Gaining a settlement in a parish was dependent on a number of criteria including being born there, having worked there for a year, serving an apprenticeship or having paid rates. Most parish officials kept evidence of parishioners' settlements as it saved money in future claims and provided evidence in disputed cases.

These documents can, therefore, provide us with autobiographical details of our ancestors we are unlikely to find in many other sources. The types of information recorded are age and place of birth, parish of residence, details of marriage and children, employment or apprenticeships served, and the value of the property they lived in. As a place of settlement was taken from a father, for children unless they were illegitimate, and from a husband, for married women, they can also tell us a husband's or father's details in the case of widows, deserted wives and destitute children.

The settlement examination taken for Thomas Smith, a gardener living in Weybread in Suffolk in 1817, was very comprehensive. In it he describes who he worked for over the previous twenty-five years and the wages and clothing he received. This includes time working in different parts of Suffolk, London and Norfolk, and how his job in London came to an end when his employer's business failed. He also mentions family members and who they were married to, as he spent time staying with them. Finally he tells how he was 'drawn for the Militia' and served in the East Suffolk Regiment for about three weeks, and when he married.

Settlement certificates tell us which parish a person belonged to at the time they were taken. They can tell us occupations and ages, wives', husbands' and childrens' names and a woman's marital status.

Overseers and churchwardens account books record both payments to paupers and money received from local ratepayers towards the poor rates. They may also include the costs involved in establishing a person's settlement in a parish. Some also kept lists of people who arrived in their parish with a certificate from elsewhere. For example, the borough records for Great Yarmouth include lists of paupers examined at their place of settlement between 1756 and 1855. These include people's names, where they belonged and whether or not they were removed. For instance, when Ann

Miller was examined in November 1797, her settlement was found to be in the parish of St James, Bury St Edmunds and she was removed.

Removal orders give the date of the order, sometimes occupations and ages, marital status for a woman, children's names and sometimes ages, and where they were being removed to. Sometimes other details may be added regarding proof of settlement or the costs of removal. If the order was overturned it would be cancelled, whilst disputed cases could be referred to the local courts (usually the Quarter Sessions).

Bastardy papers refer to the collection of records relating to maintenance for illegitimate children. If a woman had a child she could not support, the parish officials examined her to find out who the father was. When Ann Bennett had two illegitimate children, first by Thomas and then William Whiter, in North Elmham in the early 1800s both men were ordered to pay towards her 'lying in' and maintenance for their children.

Lots of examples of what the different type of poor law records can tell you can be found at the following website. Although referring to Derbyshire, the information given applies to other counties including those in East Anglia.

www.homepages.rootsweb.ancestry.com/~spire/Yesterday/index.htm

Large numbers of these records have been indexed and/or transcribed, and all four East Anglian counties have copies in various formats.

Essex Record Office has copies of the indexes produced by the local family history society to examinations, removal orders, settlement certificates, apprenticeship and bastardy papers from the 1600s to the mid-1800s.

Again, Cambridgeshire Family History Society has another of their excellent online databases for these records. This is for settlement papers, pauper apprenticeships and bastardy agreements from 1604 to 1860. This can also be accessed in the record office search rooms.

The card indexes at the three record offices in Suffolk cover the period circa 1600–1850. The references are taken from parish poor law records and include settlement examinations, removal orders, settlement certificates, bastardy examinations and bonds, plus apprenticeship records. Many of these can also be found on A2A.

Norfolk Record Office has a variety of indexes and transcripts dating from around 1600 on card and printed indexes, and on their online catalogue. Although these are mostly removal orders, settlement certificates and examinations, other parish records are gradually being added to their online catalogue. There is some duplication between the different lists as they have not yet been fully amalgamated, so each set of indexes needs checking.

Each record office in the region has individual listings for each parish and the records which belong to it. These often include brief details of the names and other relevant information of the people recorded in bastardy papers, settlement certificates and removal orders. An example from the lists of parish records for Weybread in Suffolk is this settlement certificate which summarizes the main details from this document:

John Reeve, miller, age 31 years, wife Mary age 30 yrs and their children John age 4 yrs and James age 6 mths, of Brome, Nfk. 36 June 1780.

Although the majority of records of the poor exist as documents in their own right, it is also possible to find references to the poor in other records. The flyleaf of a parish register for Houghton next Harpley in Norfolk contains a memoranda referring to three vagrants in 1696. Among them 'Robert Bell aged 21 was taken up as a Vagrant Rogue & whipped according to Law & a Passe made him to passe to Hemswell in Lincolnshire', whilst the burial entry in Castle Acre for Hannah Howard in 1738 says she was a 'Traveller with Her Son a Blind Bag pipe man from New Castle upon Tine'. Another reference in the Castle Acre registers for 1737 indicates that not all claimants were in genuine need. The clerk has commented about Thomas Hunsley that he was 'a Blind Beggar, but one that can see to get Money and Build a House by his Trade and by his fiddle'.

Quarter Sessions and Petty Sessions court records often record removal orders, settlement decisions and bastardy orders, especially if they were disputed. For example, Charity, Ellender and Joyce Lee were all convicted of vagrancy at Swaffham Quarter Sessions in April 1793. In July the same year Ellender, Joyce, and a Varche Lee were ordered to be removed to Marden in Kent. Another instance is the summons filed in Essex Quarter Sessions in 1830 to a John Smith of West Bergholt to give evidence regarding an appeal concerning the settlement of John Wade and his family.

One helpful index is the calendars to disputed settlements which were referred to the Essex Quarter Sessions courts for the period 1827 to 1835, which are held at Essex Record Office.

Newspapers regularly carried advertisements from parish officials such as the one in the *Norfolk Chronicle* in May 1836 about John Sparkes of Taverham, which says that he had absconded, leaving his wife and family chargeable to the parish. It includes a description of him and what he wore and offered a reward for further information.

6.2 Bringing it to Life

Framlingham Castle in Suffolk had almshouses and a parish workhouse built within its walls under a bequest in the will of Sir Robert Hitcham, dated 1636. White's trade directory of 1854 refers to the almshouses as being occupied by:

> …six poor men and six poor women (widows and widowers) who have each 6s. per week, a yearly supply of clothing and coals, and medical assistance when required.

It remained a parish workhouse until 1839, when a Union Workhouse was built in Wickham Market. It is now the visitors' centre for the castle and an exhibition called 'From Powerhouse to Poorhouse' explores the history of the people who lived in the castle since it was built.

Gressenhall Farm and Workhouse Museum near East Dereham in Norfolk is also featured in the workhouse section below. However, it was originally built as a parish workhouse in the late 1770s and its displays and living history re-enactments include much about this earlier period.

It is, however, the tales these documents tell us about our ancestors' lives that bring them to life. A number of examples have been used throughout this book because they illustrate how one resource can be used to find out more, in a wider sense. I have, therefore, just used the 1817 settlement examination of John Cage from the Fakenham parish records here, as it tells us so much more than the fact he was in need of poor relief:

> Examination of John Cage now residing in the Parish of Saint Margaret in the said Borough Labourer Fifth June 1817. Who saith, That he is about Fifty nine Years of Age and was born in Grimstone in the said County as he hath been informed and believes. That at about the age of thirteen years to the best of his recollection he was hired Apprentice for seven years to Edmund Seppings of Fakenham in the said County Blacksmith which time he duly served always sleeping in his said Master's house That immediately after the expiration of his said Apprenticeship he came to Kings Lyn aforesaid where he worked at his business about four years by the weeks That since his said Apprenticeship he hath done no Act whatever to gain a settlement elsewhere, And that he now stands in need of Parochial Relief.

BOROUGH OF King's-Lynn, IN THE County of Norfolk

The EXAMINATION of John Cage now residing in the Parish of Saint Margaret, in the Borough aforesaid, Labourer taken upon Oath this Fifth Day of June One Thousand Eight Hundred and seventeen before Robert Green Esq. Mayor, and ~~Esq. Alderman,~~ ~~Two~~ one of his Majesty's Justices of the Peace of and for the said Borough, ~~One whereof is of the Quorum:~~

WHO saith, That he is about fifty nine Years of Age, and was born at Grimstone in the said County as he hath been informed and believes

That at about the age of thirteen years to the best of his recollection he was bound Apprentice for seven years to Edmund Seppings of Fakenham in the said County Blacksmith which time he duly served always sleeping in his said Masters house That immediately after the expiration of his said Apprenticeship he came to Kings Lynn aforesaid where he worked at his business about four years, by the week That since his said Apprenticeship he hath done no Act whatever to gain a Settlement elsewhere, and that he now stands in need of parochial Relief

the mark of
×
John Cage

Sworn at the Borough of King's Lynn aforesaid, the Day and Year above written.
Before
Robert Green
Mayor

Settlement Examination of John Cage, 1817. (NRO: PD 204/80/90)

Chapter Seven

WORKHOUSES

The Poor Law Amendment Act of 1834 abolished the parish-based system and organized English and Welsh parishes into Poor Law Unions, each with its own Union Workhouse.

There was also an almost universal belief amongst certain authorities by the 1830s, that parish relief was an easy option for people who did not want to work. It was believed that by making life in the workhouse as off-putting as possible only those in most need would use it. The underlying principle was that those capable of work should work. In this way, apart from the sick and disabled, who were therefore not responsible for their misfortune, poverty became seen as a social disgrace so awful as to be almost criminal.

In response, the Government set up a Royal Commission in 1832 to investigate the problems and propose radical changes. Although introduced in 1834, the workhouse system is often seen as a typical example of the social, economic and political changes of the Victorian era (beginning in 1837), and frequently equated with a drive for efficiency and modernization.

The Commission's report resulted in the Poor Law Amendment Act of 1834, which abolished the parish based system and organized English and Welsh parishes into Poor Law Unions, each with its own Union Workhouse. Ireland and Scotland had their own systems, beginning in 1838 and 1845 respectively. Although some existing workhouses were taken over, the majority were built from scratch.

The Poor Law Amendment Act created a central body called the Poor Law Commission for England and Wales. There was a layer of hierarchy below them with the following responsibilities:

Hierarchy	Roles & Responsibilities
The Poor Law Commission had 3 commissioners.	Responsible for forming unions of parishes for the purposes of poor relief.
Poor Law Unions Groups of parishes responsible for maintaining the poor within a wider area than just their own parish.	Administered by boards of guardians elected by open ballot of ratepayers and property owners in each parish.
Boards of Guardians	Although an elected position this was subject to a property qualification as they had to occupy property rated at £40 per year.
Board of Guardians	Although subject to the supervision of the Poor Law Commission, they had considerable autonomy.
Justices of the Peace	Became ex-officio guardians.
Parish Officials	Still responsible for maintaining those in receipt of out-relief – mainly the elderly and sick.
Parish Ratepayers	Paid towards maintaining their union workhouse.
Paupers	Most received relief within a workhouse Workhouses continued to remove paupers to other Unions until 1876.

Richard Cobbold, the rector of Wortham in Suffolk, was chaplain to the workhouse for his area. In his history of the village he frequently condemns the treatment of the poor under the workhouse system, such as the time the bed and bedding was removed from some poor old paupers and taken to the workhouse at Christmas time without any provision being made for the removal of the paupers themselves. He commented further:

It is all very well for well-to-do men of education to say that none but the worst characters should go into a Union House. How few Gentlemen have ever known what it is to toil for the bread they eat.

Outdoor relief was now only meant to be available to those who, due to age or disability, were unable to work and were, therefore, allowed to stay out of the workhouse. An example of how this system operated in practice at Southrepps in Norfolk can be found in a book called *Within Living Memory: A Collection of Norfolk Reminiscences* (Norfolk Federation of Women's Institutes, 1972). In this the interviewee describes how:

> ...in the early 1880s a crude form of public assistance was carried on in a shed in the yard of the present butchers shop. Very poor widows gathered there each week to receive one and sixpence in money and a small quantity of flour.

7.1 Finding out More

An essential guide to the history of workhouses and their records is Simon Fowler's *Workhouses* (TNA, 2007).

The first place to look is the local record offices. There are too many unions to list them for the whole region, but lists and maps showing which areas were covered by each one are readily available at all the record offices and local studies libraries. Lists of unions can also be found online on the relevant county pages on the GENUKI website.

Occasionally, where the workhouse was taken over by another institution, such as a health authority or nursing home, these records may have been amalgamated but the staff will advise you if this is the case. To find out more about which parishes a workhouse covered and where their records are kept see the lists of *Poor Law Unions* by Jeremy Gibson (FFHS) and the workhouses' website at: www.workhouses.org.uk The A2A website also includes listings for the region and the county pages on GENUKI all list local unions and provide information local records.

There are obviously some variations in the way records were kept across different unions. But in general, those of use to the family historian are:

Type of Record	Information Included
Board of Guardians Minute Books	Record day-to-day business. Can include misdemeanours of inmates, punishments, staff employment, out-relief for elderly, sick and disabled people, costs of supplies, arranging of work or apprenticeships for inmates, emigration aid; funeral costs, disputes over maintenance, etc.
Admission and Discharge Registers	Lists those entering and leaving. May include parish of residence, age, marital status, death, place of burial, etc.
Orders of Removal	State which union a pauper was being removed to. Can contain biographical information.
Settlement Examinations	Biographical account taken to find out where a pauper belonged.
Orders for Medical Relief	Type of medical aid given, for how long and costs.
Maintenance Orders under 1845 Bastardy Act	Include father's details and details of payments made.
Religious Creed Registers	Details religious creed, when admitted, from where and who gave the information.
Birth, Baptismal, Death and Burial Registers	May include details of 'home' parish.
Indoor Relief Grants Registers or Case Books	Details relief given in a workhouse, types of food, clothing, etc.
Out Relief Payments or Case Books	Details relief given to those not resident, including place of residence, amount of money, food, clothing, etc.
Paupers' next-of-kin	Biographical information.
Children under control of the Guardians	Biographical information including how they came under the workhouse control.

Children boarded out	Biographical information, plus where boarded and costs.
Leave of absence	Reasons why, and the place pauper given leave of absence to.
Vaccination Registers	List children's date of birth, parent(s) names, home parish and date of vaccination.
Clothing	Allocation of clothing allowances. May include provision for young adults leaving for work or an apprenticeship.
Assisted Emigration	Various government schemes offering financial assistance to emigrate. Some financial assistance from individual unions.
Letter Books	Copies of references for staff, letters to other unions re. settlement and/or costs of paupers from other areas. May include letters to local businesses and organizations.

The survival of workhouse records is very variable. For example, whilst the minutes of Guardians' meetings for Essex usually survive from 1834, there are few other records before the late nineteenth century.

Examples from some of these records show the variety of information which can be discovered. One is the case of David Birt who was born in the Woodbridge Union Workhouse in Suffolk in 1861. The birth registers for this workhouse record him as illegitimate and as chargeable to the parish of Pettistree.

Numerous examples could be included here from the Guardian minute books, but those for the Docking Union include some illuminating entries about provision for the ill and disabled. For instance, entries in May 1840 and 1841 for the Wagg family, of Bircham Magna, build a picture of one family's experiences. The first entries recorded that John Wagg was 57 years of age with a wife and three children. On 27 May 1840 entries for the same family state 'one of them an idiot, the woman is ill' and granted them relief to the amount of six pence and one stone of flour. It also noted that an application to have the 'idiot' admitted was dismissed for the present. Further entries in October 1841 only refer to two children in this family, and state that 'one of

Docking Union Workhouse in the 1920s.

them an Idiot, the man is infirm, to have 1/6 & 2 Stone of flour for one week'. In November the family was admitted to the workhouse and the guardians authorized that John and his wife, who were described as infirm, to be allowed tea and sugar, and for them to be together.

Other useful workhouse records are punishment books, vaccination records, assisted emigration, out-relief payments which include place of residence, and the amount of money, food and clothing given, children under control of the Guardians, children boarded out, leave of absence and letter books. The letter books, for instance, can include anything from copies of references for staff members and letters to other unions, regarding settlements and the costs of paupers from other areas, to local businesses and organizations regarding workhouse business.

References to people in receipt of poor relief can be found in other sources. The 1901 census, for instance, shows George and Rebecca Palmer living on the High Street, Harlow and listed as in 'receipt of parish relief'.

Parish records still include some details of poor relief after 1834 as details of out-relief can often be found among churchwardens' and overseers' accounts.

Parish registers frequently include references to the baptisms and burials of inmates from the local workhouse. The Holme Hale burial registers for

1871, for instance, include an entry for 81 year old Thomas Cadge. On this he is described as of 'Swaffham Union House late Holm Hale. Buried in Burial Ground of Union House'.

Trade directories list local institutions such as the references in the 1870s to an 'orphan asylum containing 404 people' which had been erected in Wanstead parish between 1841 and 1851.

Newspapers carried various reports regarding workhouses such as staff appointments, advertisements from the workhouse guardians for tenders for supplies, visits from local dignitaries or Christmas meals enjoyed by the inmates.

7.2 Bringing it to Life

The first mention must go to the fantastic Workhouses website. This includes most of the East Anglian workhouses and details their history with photographs and a range of general information about the inmates and workers taken from official reports, newspapers and other sources at www.workhouses.org.uk

The former Mitford and Launditch Union Workhouse and Farm at Gressenhall in Norfolk is now a museum. Among the many original features, from its time as a workhouse, are the old people's cottage and punishment cell.

Poppyland Publishing has published a history of the Gressenhall Farm and Workhouse. Poppyland's website has a Support and Resources link that lists inmates and other people associated with this workhouse. Also included is general information on the workhouse buildings with an interactive plan at www.poppyland.co.uk

Chapter Eight

CHARITIES AND HEALTHCARE

Extensive collections of local and national charities, established hundreds of years ago, still exist today. Many of our ancestors received assistance from these charities in the form of money, clothing, fuel, healthcare, educational provision or the arranging of apprenticeships. A typical example is the Worlingham coal charity in Suffolk which provided 'coals, wood or other fuel for the poor of the parish'.

8.1 Charities

Records relating to charities and healthcare at a local level are frequently intertwined with those for the poor. Until the mid-nineteenth century most charities were locally based and, therefore, limited to individual villages, trades and occupations, or to certain groups such as old widows or orphans. The concept of giving to those less well-off was strongly ingrained, and it was common for people to leave charitable bequests in their wills.

When William Nobbs received a grant from the Norman Foundation towards his school uniform costs in 1945, he was one in a long line of recipients of a charity dating back to the early 1700s. Still in operation today through local solicitors, this foundation was established under the will of Alderman John Norman of Norwich who left bequests in trust specifically to provide for the education of his relations. Once the school closed the trust gave grants to descendants of his relatives, usually for the purchase of uniforms, books and equipment.

Many benefactors simply added to existing schemes or left it up to the discretion of the churchwardens and overseers of a parish as to how a bequest was used. Others endowed specific charities such as almshouses, hospitals and schools. As most were administered by local parish, borough, town and city officials many references can still be found amongst parish records.

When locally born Thomas Cook died in Pentonville in Middlesex in 1811, he gave numerous bequests to charities, almshouses and hospitals in Norfolk and Suffolk, many of which were in places he had lived, or had family and trade connections. One was for bank annuities of £700 to be used:

> …for the benefit and relief of the Four Almspeople for the time being living and residing in the Almshouses situate in or near a certain place called South Lynn Plain of Fynnkell Row and usually called or known by the name of Vallingers Almshouses in the Parish of South Lynn All Saints.

Thomas Cook also left a similar bequest of £6,600 to local almshouse, Doughty's Hospital. This continued a long standing family connection to this hospital dating back to when a Thomas and Robert Cook founded Cook's Almshouses in the 1690s. This subsequently became part of Doughty's Hospital.

Much information on the founding of Cook's Almshouses and Doughty's Hospital can be found in publications, including *The Mayors of Norwich, 1403–1835.* (Cozens, Hardy & Kent, 1938). References to the distribution of charitable bequests from members of the Cook family are also to be found in the parish records of places left money. When he died in 1703, Robert was described in contemporary accounts as the richest man in Norwich, a wealth which had been founded on the wool trade. The wills of these men also reveal numerous other charitable bequests, in particular gifts to the poor of various parishes. As usually occurred with large estates the details of Thomas Cook's will in 1811 were widely reported in local newspapers.

The types of assistance and charities to be found include anything from the upkeep of a church, purchasing bells or pews, schools, the provision and upkeep of almshouses or hospitals, food, and coal or turfs for the old and sick. One of the most popular was that made towards the costs of arranging apprenticeships for boys and girls. This was because apprenticeships were seen as a practical method of assisting people out of poverty through work.

Contributions often came from guilds and individuals associated with those trades.

8.1.1 Finding out More

Details of those still in existence can be accessed via the Charity Commissioners. Archive collections for national charities can be found via The National Archives or A2A.

From 1812 the Clerk of the Peace usually kept records of charitable trusts, noting the names of trustees and the charity's objects, investments and income. This means there may be references to these amongst local Quarter Sessions records.

Between 1832 and 1834 the incumbents of each parish had to make a return to the government of charities in their parish stating by whom and when they were founded and for what purpose. Most local record offices have preserved the earliest examples for historical interest, plus any that are particularly detailed. A set of the annual returns of the William Bulwer Trust for 1832–35 in the parish of Wood Dalling in Norfolk, describes this charity as receiving a rent charge of £6.10 bequeathed in the 1658 will of Edward Bulwer. Later additions to the fund from other beneficiaries are also described as being for the benefit of the poor not receiving parish relief.

As mentioned, under the section on parish records, it is possible to find details of the administration of local charities among the records originally held in the parish chest. The parish records for Wood Dalling show this as being a scheme of the Charity Commissioners, dated 1898, relating to the charity mentioned above. This describes how the charity should be run and the income distributed and who the trustees were. Another parish record relating to this charity is the Vicars' account book, 1885–1936 which lists recipients of this fund and how much they received.

Trade Directories include lists of local charities. These were mostly taken from the *Reports of the Commission for Inquiring Concerning Charities* published between 1819 and 1840, which attempted to record all charities in the country. The commission recorded who the benefactor was, their will or deed of settlement, the charity's trustees, property or income. Numerous examples of these can be found, such as the entry in White's 1844 directory of Suffolk for Stonham Parva which describes several charities including:

In 1523, Margaret Gowle left about 15 acres of land in Chilton, for charitable uses in Little Stonham; and it is now let for £20 a year, which is distributed in winter, in coals, by the churchwardens among the poor parishioners.

8.2 Healthcare

The healthcare people received until relatively recently was largely dependent on ability to pay. Although the majority of care took place within the home, there have been hospitals and other institutions caring for the sick, elderly and disabled for centuries. Many early hospitals were monastic or charitable foundations. Although many were closed when the monasteries were dissolved, others were subsequently established by universities, charities, parish officials, workhouses and individuals. One such example is the Great Hospital in Norwich which is an almshouse founded in 1249 still providing care for elderly residents today.

Whilst some hospitals and asylums were purpose built, others have had more than one use in their lifetime. Many workhouse infirmaries became hospitals as workhouses were phased out. Inmates from Thorpe Asylum in Norwich were transferred to a hospital in Suffolk while the hospital was used a rehabilitation hospital for wounded servicemen. Some large private houses

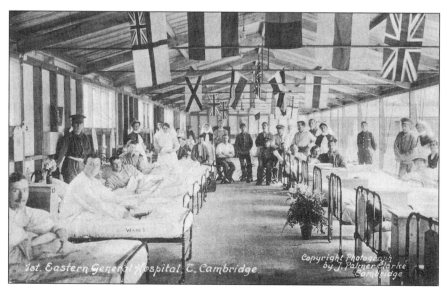

Cambridge 1st Eastern General Hospital at the end of the First World War.

were also used as hospitals in wartime such as Stansted Hall in Essex which was used a hospital by the British Red Cross during the Second World War.

8.2.1 Finding out More

Again, there are a variety of sources which can supply information about healthcare in the past. Descriptions of health problems and disabilities can also be found amongst these. One of the most accessible are census returns as these recorded some details about physical and mental disabilities from 1851 onwards in a separate column. The section for occupation may also record whether someone was an 'annuitant' or in receipt of poor relief, while additional details regarding disabilities are also occasionally entered in this section.

There are a several foundations and charities that specifically dealt with orphaned, abandoned or pauper children. The majority of records for these are kept in their own archives. However, such children often ended up in the care of the parish and parish records may include details of churchwardens putting them out to nurse and later arranging apprenticeships. References can also turn up in other locations such as court records.

Hospital administrative records are closed to the public for thirty years, whilst patient records are closed for 100 years. Although many older records have been destroyed there are still some wide ranging collections relating to hospitals, asylums and sanatoriums in local record offices, including those of staff and patients. The National Archives and the Wellcome Institute have collaborated on a hospital records project to build a database cataloguing the records of over 1,000 hospitals since 1660 at: www.nationalarchives.gov.uk/hospitalrecords

There are a few indexes and transcripts to hospital records. One example is an index to women in the British Lying In Hospital in London from Huntingdonshire and Cambridgeshire. This was produced by the Cambridgeshire Family History Society and a copy can be seen in both record offices. An example from this is the reference to Antonnetta Mayes of Manley in 1803. This says she was 37 and the wife of William, a labourer. This hospital was established in 1749 to cater for distressed and poor women, especially the wives of soldiers and sailors. The original records are now held at the London Metropolitan Archives and include particulars of patients from 1749–1868 and birth and baptismal registers from 1749–1830 (Ref. H14/BLI).

The Access to Archives website has listings for local archives of hospital records, some of which include some details of individuals. References on this to the Warley Hospital for the mentally ill in Essex, for example, describe the records that are held at Essex Record Office as well as give summaries of entries in the minute books such as expenses relating to the escape of patients in 1879, payments from the benevolent fund, staff being fined or fired, advertisements for staff, reports into patient deaths and inquests, and correspondence regarding inmates.

One of the most useful series of records are the admission registers and case files, some of which include photographs. An entry in the admission registers for Thorpe St Andrew Hospital in 1873 for Susanna Cage, for example, tells us that she was aged 25 and a malsters wife from Diss. It also states she was chargeable to the Depwade Union and that she was admitted because of puerperal mania, from which she had suffered for a month. Later entries show Susanna was readmitted for the same reason on several occasions.

Trade Directories are immensely useful for finding out what healthcare provision there was in an area. References to Essex Hall in Colchester describe it as having been originally built as a railway hotel. This being unsuccessful it became the Eastern Counties Asylum for the 'care and training of idiots and imbeciles belonging to Essex, Suffolk, Norfolk and Cambridgeshire'. Originally the patients were admitted by votes of subscribers to the hospital at half-yearly elections, a limited number for life and the majority for terms of five years. Patients from elsewhere could be admitted by payment. A description of the County Lunatic Asylum at Brentwood refers to its landscaped gardens in 120 acres, with part used as a cemetery, and part as a farm and garden cultivated by patients.

Quarter Sessions records also mention lunatic asylums as they were responsible for licensing them following the County Asylums Acts of 1808, which enabled each county to build asylums for the insane, and of 1828 which gave the Secretary of State powers to send inspectors to any asylum.

The published census reports note any major changes in numbers of people in an area between each census and their contributory causes. Those for Cambridgeshire for 1921 for instance stated that a: 'large increase in population of Papworth Everard Civil Parish is attributed to the erection and occupation of a tuberculosis colony'.

Vaccination registers can also be very informative. Because of the smallpox epidemics of 1837–1840 and 1870–1872 vaccination was provided by workhouse guardians from 1840, and was compulsory for all infants from 1853 to 1948. Certificates were given to parents which usually noted the child's name and sometimes age, date of birth and details of the father and his occupation.

Older vaccination registers often survive locally among workhouse records or local authority records. In Suffolk, for example, there are several listed among workhouse records, such as the officers' report book for the Woodbridge Poor Law Union held at Bury St Edmunds, which dates from 1915 to 1931. There is also a collection, from what was the Norwich City Council Health Authority for the period 1882 to 1948, at the Norfolk office. The Norwich Health Authority collection also includes registers of all births within the city from October 1904 to December 1961 (except 1909) and deaths from 1894 to 1962.

References to vaccination also occur elsewhere. For example, the Quarter Sessions records for Essex include an order in 1838 for the vaccination of all willing prisoners in Springfield Gaol.

Occasionally, information on causes of death can turn up in burial registers as occurred in Methwold for several years from 1874 onwards.

Coroners' records can reveal an enormous amount regarding the health problems leading to someone's death. These two examples from the Norwich inquests for 1712 also illustrate how informative these can be about wider social conditions. When 27 year old John Markall died, while in prison for debt, his inquest stated he had 'for some time past had been in a deep consumption' and declared it a visitation of God. Margaret Latten, on the other hand, died at the age of 25, 'Whilst taking "physick" with Mary Levett, to cure themselves of the "itch", they both took some powder of Mary Pooley, none of them knowing it was yellow arsenic'.

The card indexes at the three Suffolk offices include numerous death notices as well as details of news reports into epidemics such as smallpox and cholera. These show once again how useful newspapers can be in discovering more information. The online transcripts on the GENUKI Suffolk, to the death notices in the *Beccles and Bungay Weekly News* show items such as the death of Mary Lock, widow of Samuel, in the Loddon and Clavering Union Workhouse in 1862 at the age of 105. This reveals that, despite being blind and deaf, she enjoyed her faculties to the last. Newspaper reports into inquests and accidents, and obituaries and death notices, can add much more detail.

Although not strictly a health issue the incidents of body snatching were a related phenomenon. Cases were reported across the region at various times, presumably for the purposes of dissection. Reports into the case of

Elizabeth Watts who was buried in Lakenham in November 1830 also reveals how precarious life was during this period, as it was only discovered that her body had been taken, when her brother died later the same month and was to be buried with his sister.

Local newspapers also reported an interesting dispute over the issue of dissection in 1872, when the guardians of the Norwich workhouse had a 'long and acrimonious discussion, before agreeing to the request of a Professor Humphrey, of Cambridge to supply him with the bodies of unclaimed persons who had died in the workhouse for the purposes of dissection'.

Some fascinating insights into wider health issues can be found in parish records and monumental inscriptions. The controversial issue of inoculation has a long history dating back to the early 1700s. A local initiative is recorded in a memorandum in the parish registers for Thorpe Market which noted the inoculations of paupers with cowpox in 1805 paid for by a local benefactress. A sad reference is the monument on the wall of Tacolneston church which says:

> Thomas Knipe Gobbett, son of the abovesaid Knipe Gobbett and Jane his wife, daughter of Thomas Woode, Esq, late of Bracon Ash, died of the small-pox by inoculation, 12th April, 1762, in the fourth year of his age.

8.3 Bringing to Life

There are numerous examples of buildings and structures associated with charities, almshouses and hospitals across the region. Some have been converted into other uses whilst others, such as the Great Hospital in Norwich, are still in use as residential and sheltered accommodation, but allow visits on designated open days each year.

A pump, erected in 1853 by Mary Gee in thanks for the absence of cholera in the village at Pound Green close to Earls Colne in Essex, stands as a reminder of the importance of clean water.

Many almshouse buildings such as the one in Eye in Suffolk still survive today. Whilst some have become private houses, others retain their links with the past as accommodation for the elderly.

Every Sunday, in Castle Rising in Norfolk, the elderly women residents of almshouses founded by Henry Howard, Earl of Northampton in 1614, process from their home in Bede House to the church dressed in long scarlet

Almshouses in Eye in Suffolk.

cloaks emblazoned with the badge of the Howard family. Once a year on Founder's Day they add a tall crowned hat, typical of the Jacobean period. One of the conditions of being a resident is regular Sunday attendance, whilst others are to be able to read and be at least 56 years old.

Chapter Nine

MIGRATION

There has always been migration to and from East Anglia, either through necessity, work and trade opportunities, or simply a desire to create a better life. Movement out of the region occurred at all levels of society and was both voluntary and involuntary. The latter includes the transportation of criminals which is included in the section on crime. As East Anglia was primarily a rural region, what follows is mainly a focus on the migration of rural workers, in particular the high levels of movement outwards in the nineteenth century.

Far flung destinations like the 'New World' have always been attractive to adventurous souls, as when the Puritans left England in response to religious persecution in the seventeenth century.

Large numbers of East Anglians were among the waves of pioneering settlers. Among the more high profile names that could be listed are men such as Bartholomew Gosnold who was born at Otley Hall in Suffolk. In 1602, he sailed to America where he named Cape Cod and Martha's Vineyard. In 1607 he was responsible for establishing the first English settlement in America at Jamestown, Virginia. Thomas Cornwallis, who played a leading role in the founding of the province of Maryland in America, was another man with local connections. He became the richest man in the colony, holding major government posts and at one point was the tenth largest exporter of tobacco to England. He later returned to England, taking up residence in Burnham Thorpe where he died in 1676.

Nevertheless, most migration was internal until the late nineteenth and early twentieth centuries. As A C Edwards points out in his history of Essex, whilst the rural population was very mobile in the eighteenth century, most movement of poor villagers was within a fairly small radius, being dependent on the yearly hiring fairs and apprenticeships. This can be seen in settlement papers and apprenticeship records for all four counties which indicate the majority of movement took place in and around the market towns where the arranging of work and other business took place. For example, the 1802 settlement examination of Elizabeth Clarke, taken in Thetford St Peter, shows she had moved from Ixworth just over the border in Suffolk, whilst the 1828 settlement certificate of Maria Potter in Ashwellthorpe says she belonged to the nearby parish of Forncett St Peter. The indexes to settlement examinations at Essex Record Office show similar patterns. When searching for references to the name Gray, out of the four people included between 1743 and 1810, all except one had a settlement within the county. A similar pattern can be seen in the indexes to settlement certificates with Michael Gray and his family recorded as living in Rochford in 1786, but having a settlement in Maldon St Peter and Jane Gray recorded in South Weald in 1747 but belonged to Barking.

There were, however, still significant numbers who moved considerable distances like Robert Gray who was resident in Harwich in Essex in 1756 but had a settlement in Monkwear in Durham. Those living or working close to coastal or river ports could move greater distances due to access to maritime transport, as when Charles Cracroft from Lincolnshire was apprenticed to grocer Robert Francis in King's Lynn in 1652.

Levels of migration, and the destinations people moved to, were affected by social and economic factors. East Anglia's problems of agricultural decline and unemployment triggered waves of movement out of its rural heartlands. It, therefore, has the distinction of having populated large areas of the UK and other parts of the world. Over the course of the 1800s in particular, thousands of people migrated abroad in search of improved living conditions.

There were various assisted emigration schemes throughout the nineteenth century and into the twentieth. Government schemes for emigration began soon after the end of the wars in 1815, when transports, returning troops from Canada, were encouraged to take on passengers at low rates, whilst the land grants of the 1820s added further encouragement. Parishes, workhouse unions, charities and church organizations actively participated in these by providing assistance money to help pay for the trip.

With the great demand for labour in some parts of United States and elsewhere, assisted emigration was seen as a method of saving money in poor relief. The Poor Law Amendment Act of 1834 allowed the government to cover most of the cost for the emigrant and the availability from 1837 of free passages to Australia prompted many parishes to accept the Commissioners' offer to provide loans towards outfitting emigrants for the voyage. These assisted schemes were little used after 1847, although emigration was still very popular.

One of the prime movers in organizing the emigration of workers from Essex in the 1870s was the farm workers' union leader, Charles Jay. In the belief that workers should be prepared to move away from areas of high unemployment to find work, Jay arranged for workers from the Braintree district to move to the north of England. He also became an agent of the Queensland Government working to attract British workers to Australia. Contemporary accounts describe a party atmosphere as around 200 people he recruited, left by train in 1874 with family and friends waving flags at stations and from houses along the route.

Child migration schemes originated in the early seventeenth century to help provide cheap labour for pioneers. Many of the organizations involved were closely associated with each other. Children's charities like Dr Barnardo's and the Children's Society were involved in sending children overseas, whilst parish officials were actively involved with running local charities and were members of the local workhouse board of guardians. These, in turn, liaised with charities, as well as being involved with their own schemes.

It is not possible to do justice to the whole subject of immigration. Suffice to say that immigration is nothing new in East Anglia, with individuals and groups recorded as moving into the region as far back as records exist. As with outward migration, trade and work opportunities, and the pursuit of religious freedom, encouraged particular groups such as the Flemish cloth workers; the Walloons and Huguenots, some of which are featured under the topics of work and trade and religion. The twentieth century saw other waves from Europe, the Caribbean, India and former British colonies in Africa and elsewhere. Some had fled war and persecution, whilst others had, like their predecessors, simply pursued the opportunity of a better life.

9.1 Finding out More

Although some material relating to both internal and external migration is held at The National Archives, there is much to be found in local record offices.

Many of the sources, already referred to in this book, illustrate the movements of people, in particular parish and workhouse records. Removal orders include countless examples which could fill a book in themselves. The removal orders for orphans Sarah and Robert Dixon aged 14 and 12, from Lambeth in Surrey, in 1851, and of John Hart and his wife Mary, from Lutton in Lincolnshire, Holland in 1836, to Winfarthing demonstrate once again the distances some people moved.

Parish records provide valuable information on those who participated in assisted emigration schemes. For example, a letter to the parish officials of Sheringham from a Henry Sotham in Oxfordshire in 1835 refers to a man named Crow who had gone to North America and was sending for his wife and family to join him:

> Having met with a person name Crow that went from your parish to Ohio North America some time since, wished me to Write to you when in England for information respecting his Wife & Family, whether they had means of getting to him; he has a very good situation and a maintenance for them, could they be sent to him, from the hints he gave me I expect they are chargeable on the Parish, should that be the case, if they will find half, Crows employer will do the other, by my writing to him in America.

The accounts section of the vestry minute books for the parish of Diss refers to an assisted emigration scheme in 1844. The first mention is a notice that they will discuss the feasibility of sending William Rudd and his family to Canada. The second proposes:

> …that William Rudd his Wife and four Children be sent out as Emigrants to Canada at the expense if the Parish. According to the rules of the Poor Law Commission.

An interesting index to Cambridgeshire people recorded in the Australian Victoria gold rush of the 1850s can be found at the Cambridgeshire Family History Society. Copies can also be accessed at Cambridge Record Office and online at: www.cfhs.org.uk/Search.html

Census returns show people's movements throughout the 1900s, whilst the reports and notes, compiled by enumerators at the time, can also be illuminating. In 1841 it was noted that over 100 people had emigrated from the parish of Willingham, Cambridgeshire alone, since 1831. Copies of these reports can be found in many local reference or local studies libraries, or accessed from the Office of National Statistics website.

Although the vast majority of records relating to immigration are held at The National Archives, some references can be found locally. The Aliens Act of 1793 required all new immigrants to register with a Justice of the Peace, whilst anyone who had an immigrant living with them had to register with their parish overseer. As a result, references can be found amongst Quarter Sessions and parish records, although their survival is variable.

Parish registers and other records for coastal areas frequently include references to other nationalities and black people, as do those for places along well used travel and trade routes.

9.2 Bringing To Life

The church of St Mary in Dedham, Essex has shields on the wall depicting the *Mayflower* to commemorate links with Dedham, Massachusetts where many local people emigrated.

Essex Record Office holds several copies of PhD theses on migration, both internally and externally, with reference to the county which provide valuable insights from an academic perspective. Among these is one by Christopher Charles Pond submitted to Queen's College, Cambridge University in 1980 on migration and mobility in Eastern England in the eighteenth century. Entitled *Internal Population and Mobility in Eastern England in the Eighteenth Century*, this looks at migration within East Anglia and nearby areas through settlement examinations and certificates.

There are some local resources relating to immigration which provide an insight into the background of 'incomers'. The history of particular groups, such as the Dutch workers who drained the Fens, are featured in a range of museums and heritage centres already referred to.

Some personal accounts can be found in collections held at local record offices. Many can be found by searching for relevant topics in their card and online indexes and catalogues. One such is an illuminating insight into the flight from France of a Huguenot couple called Paul and Madelaine Turquand which can be found in a collection of papers relating to the Martineau family amongst the Octagon chapel records in Norfolk Record Office. These are entitled an 'Extract from an account of the Huguenot Turquand family from the 10th or 11th century to the year 1814' by Louis Turquand. The Martineaus were a prominent Norwich family of French

Huguenot extraction and include the writer and social reformer Harriet (1802–1876). There is no specific reference to East Anglia within the tale, so presumably its presence within these papers is because of family and trade connections. Nevertheless, it offers a personal account of relevance to anyone with Huguenot ancestry.

The annual Black History Month each October sees a range of exhibitions and features in archive centres and museums across the region.

All the oral history, sound and photographic archives in the region include contributions relating to twentieth century immigration. One such is the Suffolk Voices project, which includes oral histories from first generation immigrants from the Caribbean describing their heritage and being accepted into new communities.

Chapter Ten

LOCAL GOVERNMENT

Local government records provide fascinating insights into all aspects of our ancestors' lives. These range from how local government worked, to the way in which issues of law and order, poverty, health and social care were dealt with in local areas.

The evolvement of local government has been gradual, with a certain amount of overlap between organizations responsible for different aspects, until the late nineteenth century.

Until 1889 much local government administration was undertaken by unelected Justices of the Peace in the Court of the Quarter Sessions and parish officials. JPs dealt with criminal acts, disputes and the regulation of lands, commons and grazing. They also regulated markets, weights and measures, the sale of bread and ale, as well as the maintenance of roads, bridges, fences, ditches and waterways. Other responsibilities were the granting of licences to public houses, collecting taxes and poor rates and the administration of gaols, lunatic asylums, the county militia and police.

Although Acts of Parliament in the 1830s and 1840s extended the role of local government and made it clearer what responsibilities each local body had, parishes were still the main basis of local government in villages. As a result, records of local poor relief, rates, road upkeep and so on can also be found among the parish records of the Anglican church.

Cities and towns such as Cambridge, Ely, Chelmsford, Colchester, Bury St Edmunds, Ipswich, King's Lynn and Norwich had their own powers to govern, enact laws and keep records, often dating back to medieval times. Royal charters and other charters gave them, and other boroughs, the right to collect tolls and dues, thereby encouraging the rise of craft guilds. Records of these guilds, apprentices, freemen, market stallholders, mayors and corporations frequently survive (see Apprentices and Freemen in the Introduction).

Boroughs and corporations have also existed in some towns, especially market towns, since medieval times. The survival of borough, corporation and parish records relating to government of local affairs is variable, but the majority of those that do exist can now be found in local records offices. These include many of the records and themes referred to throughout this book such as poor law and workhouse administration, criminal records, parish apprenticeships, lists of local property owners, local charities, maintenance of highways and the collection of rates towards the money distributed.

The Great Reform Act of 1832 heralded the development of modern government in England. This abolished rotten boroughs, enfranchised the growing industrial towns as Parliamentary boroughs, increased the proportion of men eligible to vote and ended corrupt practices in Parliament. After the reform of Parliamentary constituencies, the boroughs were reformed by the Municipal Corporations Act of 1835, which made local government more democratic as it required members of town councils to be elected by ratepayers.

Subsequent government Acts improved local government organization and led to the introduction of a variety of public services and utilities. Amongst these were the grouping of parishes into Poor Law Unions (see Poor Law and Workhouse records), the Public Health Act of 1848 which established Boards of Health to regulate sewerage and the spread of diseases in towns and boroughs (see Healthcare), the opening of council cemeteries from the 1850s onwards, the creation of public parks and open spaces, slum clearance and the widening of the franchise.

By 1888 it was clear this piecemeal system could no longer cope and the 1888 Local Government Act became the first systematic attempt to impose a standardized system of local government in England. This created county councils, all run by elected councillors, who were responsible for general local government business plus the management of roads, bridges and drains.

Nevertheless, within the county councils, the parish was still the basic unit of administration until the Local Government Act of 1894 finally separated the administration of the community from that of the church at parish level, by creating parish councils which took over the churches' civil responsibilities. These civic parish councils took care of allotments, burial grounds, drainage, lighting, planning, recreation, street furniture and village halls. Further acts changed the specific functions of local government but it still remained separate from the church and court systems.

10.1 Finding out More

Any kind of administration generates paperwork, and local government records are no exception. All the local record offices have lists of surviving parish records, and all have some indexes of certain groups of records from amongst these, most notably the poor law records.

An interesting collection of parish records for Kenninghall in Norfolk is a good example of the parish system of government in practice, and the kinds of information to be found. These include poor rate books for 1835–37 containing references to local property owners. Among these is a James Burlingham who owned a house, cottage and land at Park Common. These books describe the types of properties, whether they were occupied and who the occupier was, their location, the value at which they were assessed for poor rates and the amount of poor rate to be collected at a rate of two shillings in the pound.

All the local record offices and studies libraries also have much material in their collections of borough and corporation archives dating from before the Reform Acts of the nineteenth century as well as afterwards. What is given here are some representative examples of the kinds of resources you may find that have not been looked at in more depth elsewhere in this guide.

The various Reform Acts from 1832 onwards gradually increased the numbers of people entitled to vote, with all men over 21 and women over the age of 30 finally allowed to vote in 1918. Poll books were first published in 1696 when sheriffs were required to compile lists of voters in county elections. These were usually divided by parish and list the name of each voter, and who they voted for before the introduction of the secret ballot in 1872. Once the secret ballot was introduced the poll books became redundant. There is a large collection of poll books for the whole country at the Guildhall Library in London. In East Anglia, poll books for various dates are held at Cambridgeshire, Essex and Suffolk record offices, whilst the Norfolk books are held at the heritage centre. Many have been published and these can be found at family history societies and local studies libraries.

Whilst poll books only include a small percentage of the population, they give an indication of the status of those who are listed. Those for Dunston in Norfolk in 1835 show that the candidates were Walpole, Wodehouse,

Windham and Gurney. One or sometimes two seats in Parliament were being contested and, in this case, three men are listed as voters with Walpole and Wodehouse both gaining three votes each.

Minutes of council meetings can show how, and by whom, decisions were made about the neighbourhoods in which your ancestors lived. Rent and rate records and electoral registers are often a neglected source in family history, perhaps because their financial role means they are perceived as having little genealogical relevance. However, they can provide a person's address, an indication of financial status, whether they were eligible to vote, and in what capacity, before all men and women were entitled to do so on equal terms. Later electoral registers can be used to find addresses and the names of other family members.

Electoral registers are lists of people eligible to vote in government elections from every level from parish council to Parliamentary and European. They are compiled by local authorities and divided into polling districts. Electoral registers also double as registers for local government. What this means is that some people who could not vote in Parliamentary elections (such as women before 1918) were still listed as they could still vote in local elections due to being local ratepayers.

The electoral registers for Aldeburgh in Suffolk for the 1930s, 1940s and 1950s proved very useful in narrowing down who lived in Crespigny House on Hartington Road, when it changed hands and was converted to a nursing home around 1952–53. The card indexes and catalogues at Ipswich Record Office provide further references to Crespigny House in planning, architects, legal and Social Services records between 1953 and 1990. These include re-wiring and alterations made in 1953, installation of a lift 1954 and the let of a flat in 1984.

Many local record offices and libraries have copies of electoral registers relating to their area. A national set of electoral registers from 1918 onwards can be found at the British Library. For a comprehensive listing see J Gibson and C Rogers *Electoral Registers since 1832* (FFHS, 1989). Or use the FAMILIA website at: www.familia.org.uk

Public health records dealt with living conditions and infectious diseases. Their minute books and reports provide fascinating reading and can be found in local archives. All local record offices hold these with some published reports available in reference and local studies libraries.

The Public Health Acts of 1848 and 1875 gave Borough Councils and Boards of Guardians responsibilities to initiate local Sanitary Authorities to deal with water supplies, drainage and street cleaning, and the appointment of a Medical Officer of Health became compulsory in 1909. Further powers to deal with housing schemes and unsanitary dwellings came with the 1890 Housing of the Working Classes Act and the 1909 Town Planning Act. Details of decisions made can be found in council minutes books.

Planning applications provide a history of the growth of villages, towns and cities by showing how and when houses and businesses were built, extended or altered. Objections to applications can also indicate community concerns over expansion or changing character.

The section on urbanization and housing looks at some of the records associated with housing in more detail, so here it simply suffices to say that the allocation of housing, collection of rents and rate from individuals and businesses, or details of disputes, all provide information on people's living conditions.

Licensing Sessions were often held at Petty Sessions and Quarter Sessions where decisions were made on the licensing of alehouses, cinemas, theatres, premises for public performances, the playing of music and sale of alcohol. These record the names and addresses of people applying for licences.

10.2 Bringing it to Life

Apart from the museums and heritage centres devoted to workhouse or gaol history, there are not many attractions, museums or heritage centres that focus on the day-to-day workings of local government. However, several aspects such as slum clearances can be found as small displays or features in some of the larger museums.

Some of the region's guildhalls have already been mentioned in connection with the wool trade, but are also worth looking at in the context of their role as centres for civic affairs.

Chapter Eleven

EDUCATION

Educational records before the late 1800s are very scarce, with perhaps the exception of some of the large private institutions. Many schools were originally charitable foundations with some grammar and public schools emerging from religious establishments dating back to medieval times. The Norwich School, for example, was originally the almonry of the Benedictine monastery which educated poor boys for free. This became the King Edward VI Grammar School following the Reformation and the former college and chantry of St John the Evangelist are still part of the school premises used today. Another example is the Newport Free Grammar School in Essex which was founded for poor boys by Dame Joyce Frankland in 1588 after her son fell off a horse and died in the village.

Universities were the preserve of a small minority until the mid-twentieth century. Cambridge University is one of the oldest and most prestigious universities in the country, with the first college, Peterhouse, founded in 1284. Among the many celebrated alumni are Dr John Caius, an important pioneer in the science of anatomy and benefactor of Gonville and Caius College. He was physician to Edward VI, Queen Mary and Queen Elizabeth, and is believed to be the inspiration for the character of Dr Caius in Shakespeare's *Merry Wives of Windsor*.

The first Cambridge College for women was founded in 1869, in Hitchin, by Emily Davies. It moved to Girton in 1873 to be 'near enough for male lecturers to visit but far enough away to discourage male students from doing the same'. It became a mixed college in 1983. Relations between 'town and gown' have, at times, been noted for their conflict. In the 1800s relations between the university and townsfolk were so hostile that the Vice-Chancellor appointed his own special constables to keep the peace.

Before compulsory elementary education was introduced in 1870 large numbers of people did not receive a formal education at all. Whilst some learnt how to read and write or gained other skills through serving an apprenticeship or from other work opportunities, for most, who could not afford to pay, their only chance of an education was through informal or charitable arrangements. Parson Woodforde of Weston Longville in Norfolk described one such arrangement in his diary for December 1776:

> Mr Chambers the Schoolmaster who is lately come here called on me this morning to let me know that he would teach my servants Ben and Will to write and read at 4/6d a quarter each – which I agreed for.

During the late eighteenth century the appalling conditions of child labour in both urban and rural areas had encouraged a movement which campaigned for some kind of national system of day schools. Nevertheless, there was still no uniform system, and most schools operating before the 1830s were either dame schools run from private houses, charity schools, Sunday schools and grammar schools, or public schools for those with the financial means. The quality of education offered by many of these was very variable, with the rector of Wortham in Suffolk, Richard Cobbold, commenting that the woman who kept his local dame school was 'very ignorant herself' and 'imposing rather than enlightening'.

Richard Cobbold was one of those who set up a local school, appointing a succession of schoolmasters. The schoolmaster was to teach 'the fear of God together with a competent degree of arithmetic', whilst his wife was to teach 'writing and reading, needlework and spelling'.

It was only from the 1830s and 1840s that funding on any national level was aimed at schools. One measure was the annual sum granted by Parliament in 1833 to help charities, mainly the National Society (Church of England) and British and Foreign School Society (Nonconformist), to build schools. These eventually led to the formation of an elementary school system across the country.

The Elementary Education Act, 1870 divided England and Wales into school districts, each with elected school boards. These school boards were required to provide elementary schools (known as board schools) where existing facilities were inadequate, in order that a place was available for every child requiring it. However, many schools charged fees, discouraging

Schoolchildren outside Scarning School in Norfolk in the early twentieth century.

poor parents. Acts of 1876 and 1880 prohibited children under the age of 10 being employed, and most under the age of 13 had to attend school.

Free elementary education for all children was introduced in 1891. Secondary schooling remained dominated by public and grammar schools, although some accepted poor pupils via scholarships. School boards were replaced by county council education authorities in 1902. These were given the power to provide or fund secondary education as well as elementary. The provision of secondary education became compulsory in 1918, with the school leaving age being raised to 14, then again to 15 in 1947.

11.1 Finding out More

Survival of records for ordinary schools tends to be poor before compulsory elementary education was introduced. This means the majority of records date from after 1870.

Although some records are still kept by individual schools, most regional archives have comprehensive collections of records relating to education. The majority are from local authority or denominational schools and are subject to closure rules, usually seventy-five years, to protect the confidentiality of living people who might appear in them.

School records which do survive can include plans and building details, logbooks, minutes, punishment books and photographs. As these records are mostly administrative they do not include details of every child. Log books (day books kept by the head teacher) include details of attainment and attendance of children, the school curriculum and assistant teachers at the school. The log books for Runton in Norfolk, for example, have entries in 1907 recording matters such as which children were excluded from school because of scarlet fever in the family and how bad weather affected attendance.

One of the most useful sources are the admission and discharge registers which record the names of children, their parents or guardians. The Old Hunstanton Church of England School admission books date from 1861 as it was formerly an endowed school. Entries for members of the Wagg family show that Rose Wagg was born in 1897, admitted in 1904 and left in 1913. Further information given is that her guardian was her grandfather James and the last school she attended was Great Bircham. Robert Wagg left school in 1920 because he was '14 years of age', and the discharge register includes the remark that he was 'ill from accident last month'.

Lists of pupils for many of the public schools have been printed and the Society of Genealogists has a large collection of these. Copies relating to local schools, along with any histories produced, can frequently be found in local archives and libraries, or accessed via the school concerned. Older universities such as Cambridge produce printed alumni lists.

There are a variety of other sources which can be used to find out more. Apprenticeship records, for example, may include provision for the teaching of reading and writing or particular skills associated with that trade.

Census records from 1841 onwards can reveal the whereabouts of schools, the names of resident employees and pupils who attended boarding schools.

Trade directories and gazetteers list all local schools and the names of the head teachers or owners. They also include details of those formed through charitable bequests or associated with particular religious organizations. For instance, Wilson's 1870–72 *Imperial Gazetteer of England and Wales* records a church school in the parish of Matching in Essex, whilst White's directory of 1850 describes how a free school in the Norfolk village of Feltwell was founded by Sir Edmund Mundeford in 1643. Another example is the entry in White's 1883 Norfolk directory for Overstrand. This tells us the school was endowed by Anna Gurney and her brother Hudson in 1830 and named Jonathan Betts Spencer as the local schoolmaster. The school, known to this day as the Belfry, is still the local primary school.

Newspapers include reports of exam results and the names of participants, especially those for the scholarship to grammar school later known as the 11 Plus, as when the *Norfolk Chronicle* for 9 August 1940 reported that:

> The Norfolk Education Committee have awarded 110 junior scholarships and have recommended the Governors of Secondary schools to award 183 special places. These awards will be tenable as from the beginning of the autumn term, 1940.

11.2 Bringing it to Life

The Old Library, St John's College in Cambridge, is just one of the many Cambridge colleges worth visiting as it houses an internationally important collection of personal papers, manuscripts, books and photographs.

School scrapbooks and magazines may survive, providing details of the achievements and accomplishments of pupils past and present. Many local histories include photographs of the local school and its pupils at various points in its history. One example is a photographic history published by the Cambridgeshire Family History Society entitled *Gamlingay: Portrait of an English Village*.

Occasionally an educational institution becomes known to the wider world. This was the case with Burston in Norfolk. It became famous for the longest strike in history staged by local children in support of the village schoolteachers, Tom and Kitty Higdon, who were sacked primarily for coming into conflict with the school authorities and local farmers over children being taken out of school to work. The strike began in 1914 and lasted for twenty-five years, and included villagers opening their own school in 1917. During that time the 'Strike School' received world wide support. The school still stands on the village green and is now a museum and the centre of an annual rally commemorating the strike every April. *The Burston School Strike* by B Edwards (Lawrence and Wishart, 1974) incorporates many contemporary accounts from participants, official and newspaper reports in this history of the strike.

Chapter Twelve

RAILWAYS

The coming of the railways had an effect on every area of life, from work and leisure to housing developments. Until the mid-nineteenth century sea ports shipped produce, and wherries and barges carried loads inland on rivers and canals such as the Stort Navigation to Bishops Stortford along the Essex and Hertfordshire border. Roads were poor, but wagons were able to use them and livestock were walked from many parts of East Anglia to markets and fairs and south to London, whilst cattle drovers came into the region from as far away as Scotland.

The development of the railway system had a phenomenal impact on nineteenth century Britain. In 1830 there were less than 100 miles of railway open. By 1852 there were 6,600 miles and by 1901, when Queen Victoria died, the total route mileage had almost trebled. Railway services to coastal areas helped transform places like Clacton-on-Sea and Southend-on-Sea in Essex into popular seaside resorts, a popularity that was boosted even further with the introduction of bank holidays in 1871.

The effects of railway development on the market town of Wisbech can be taken as an example of the impact on trade in numerous towns and villages across the region. Despite being twelve miles from the sea, Wisbech was a prosperous port in the early nineteenth century. Its agricultural prosperity attracted the building of railways at an early date. The Eastern Counties Railway opened a short branch in 1847 followed by the Anglian Railway. These later joined to form the Great Eastern Railway (GER) and the two lines were joined to permit through running. A third line was built by the Peterborough, Wisbech and Sutton Bridge Railway (later the Midland and Great Northern Joint Railway).

All these lines carried fruit and vegetables to the markets of London and the Midlands. The GER later secured the support of the Board of Trade to build a light tramway linking Wisbech to Upwell and Outwell, because it brought the railway to a place that would not be economical with a normal line. The first stretch opened in 1883 and the subsequent 1896 Light Railway Act was partly due to its success.

The tramway benefited the canal that ran between Wisbech and Upwell in its early years, as large quantities of coal were shipped to Outwell then offloaded into barges for transport elsewhere in the Fens. However, the success of the tramway was ultimately responsible for the canal's demise in 1914 as a viable trade route. Whilst the tramway was not profitable in its own right, it supported the freight and passenger traffic on the main line. By 1949 eight trips were leaving Upwell on weekdays and three on Saturdays during the fruit season but, like many others affected by Beeching's Axe, it closed in 1966.

The Light Railways Act of 1896 was passed in response to the agricultural depression of the late nineteenth century. This act intended to reduce distress in the countryside. The relaxing of the rules governing the building of railways was to be allowed if farming would benefit or a link was made between a fishing harbour and a market, or to support 'some definite industry'. Three light railways were built in Essex. One of these, the Kelvedon and Tollesbury Railway, known as the 'Crab and Winkle' line, was completed in 1904, carrying both freight and passengers. Among those who championed its construction was Arthur C Wilkin, whose Britannia Fruit Preserving company at Tiptree stood to benefit from easier freight transport. A link between sea and rail was planned and a pier extension at Tollesbury was built, although this only lasted a few years. Shrimp were one of the cargo carried during that time. It carried passengers until 1952, before finally closing in 1962.

In East Anglia, Essex was the most affected by the growth of the railway network as it brought London closer, radically altering the rural nature of those areas closest to the metropolis. As well as transforming the transport system the railways offered work opportunities to thousands. The number of people employed on the railways in Essex increased from 408 in 1851 to 10,958 in 1901. This compared with an increase in Cambridgeshire between 1851 and 1901 from 310 to 2,369 people. Whilst the work was frequently hard, there were many benefits such as pensions and sick pay. In addition to

The new railway station at Romford, Essex in 1937.

drivers, engineers and signal men, there were 60,000 railway clerks in England by the beginning of the twentieth century.

The Grays from Stratford were one of many, who had several members of the same family working on the railways. The census returns show that Henry William moved into Stratford in the 1870s where he spent the rest of his life working for the London and North Eastern Railway (LNER) as a boiler maker's assistant. His three sons, Joseph, Harold and Richard all went to work for the same company as fitters, engine strippers and coppersmiths. The LNER was the second biggest of the four private companies which had merged after the First World War and were responsible for creating the *Flying Scotsman*, which was the first non-stop express train in the UK.

The railways also had a major impact on the leisure and holiday activities of countless people. Whilst the seaside has always been a popular holiday destination for some, there is no doubt that the accessibility provided, through quick and cheap travel on trains, transformed many workday fishing villages and ports into full blown resorts where people flocked for fun and relaxation.

This can be seen in Norfolk where railways began in 1844. Cromer, for instance, had been a significant resort since the late 1700s, praised by no less

Ipswich Railway Station.

than author Jane Austen in her novel *Emma*. Nevertheless, it became a highly fashionable seaside destination rivalling Brighton in the late Victorian era when a rail link was opened between Norwich and the Midlands. The area around Cromer and Sidestrand became known as 'Poppyland' when the author Clement Scott described the area as such in a holiday article for the *Daily Telegraph* in 1883. This description was then, in turn, used to promote the area in advertisements for the rail service.

Other coastal areas also developed as resorts specifically in response to the accessibility offered by rail travel. New Hunstanton in Norfolk for example was a purpose built resort developed in the 1860s by Mr Hamon L'Estrange of Hunstanton Hall to take advantage of the railway and the growing popularity of seaside resorts.

The coastal areas of Suffolk also benefited once the first railway line opened in 1846, linking Ipswich and Bury St Edmunds to London. The success of the East Suffolk line led to rail connections to Framlingham,

Aldeburgh and Southwold. A connection to Aldeburgh from 1859 allowed more people access to the coast, both for day trippers from within Suffolk and holiday makers from London. Suffolk may also be able to claim the honours for transporting one the most unusual loads by train when a stuffed giraffe was transported by a taxidermist in London to Ipswich museum in 1909.

The growth of the railway system also encouraged the spread of housing developments as commuting to work was now viable (see Urbanization and Housing). Houses for the middle classes were built in areas like Thorpe Hamlet in Norwich, partly because it was close to the new railway station, enabling easy access to transport.

The introduction of steam-operated railways also ushered in an impressive architectural heritage. Viaducts, tunnels, bridges and railway stations illustrate a marriage between buildings designed to serve a practical function that also stand as architecturally important and influential in their own right.

12.1 Finding out More

There were a large number of small railway companies in the region such as the Clacton-on-Sea (1877–83), Ely and Huntingdon (1845–47), King's Lynn Dock and Railway (1865–1947) and the Mid-Suffolk Railway (1896–1923) which were gradually renamed or merged with others. The dominant East Anglian railway companies by the turn of the twentieth century were the General Eastern Railway (GER), the London and North Eastern Railway (LNER) and the Midland and Great Northern Joint Railway (M&GN), whose records are largely kept at The National Archives.

An index to East Anglian railway companies, with a brief summary of their history and of which companies each became a part, can be found at the UK Wagons website www.auod93.dsl.pipex.com/Companies.htm

East Anglia Railways Remembered by Leslie Oppitz (Countryside Books, 1989) is a very readable account of railway development in the region with details of what lines remain.

The Railway Family Ancestors Family History Society has a wide ranging collection of sources and information on people associated with the railway industry (see Resource Directory for contact details).

Although there is not space here to list the many railway records held at The National Archives, it is worth noting that they do have a number, such as staff and pension records. However, most of these are from the pre-nationalization railway companies and tend to be for the larger companies.

The Tracking Railways Archives Project is coordinated by the Railway and Canal Historical Society, and aims to list all railway archive collections held at locations throughout Britain. At present this is still in its infancy but details can be found at: www.trap.org.uk/FamHist.html

Local archives don't generally have records relating to specific railway companies. They do, however, have other records which relate to the purchase of land and the building of railways, including maps and plans. With the expansion of railways from the 1860s maps were drawn up for proposed routes. These detail the ownership of properties along that route. They also provide a useful insight into the routes likely to have been taken by families moving in and out of an area.

Cambridgeshire has a mixture of records, mostly filed with the Quarter Sessions. These include copies of Acts of Parliament, plans and notices to owners along proposed routes.

Other records can be found in private collections such as the estate records for Kersey in Suffolk at The King's College Archive in Cambridge. These include title deeds and papers relating to the sale of land to the Bedford and Cambridge Railway Company in 1864.

One of the most useful resources for finding out about those who worked for the railways are staff magazines and newsletters. Some can be found at the Colindale Newspaper Library, the National Railway Museum, London Transport Museum, as well as in The National Archives and record offices, local studies libraries and heritage centres.

The Essex Record Office has probably the best collection of railway material in the region. The many hundreds of documents date from the mid-1800s and include a volume recording Acts of Parliament entitled 'London, Tilbury and Southend Railway Acts, 1882 to 1904', an extract from the Great Eastern Railway Bill of 1883 showing land to be purchased in Nettleswell and Harlow, various magazines such as the *North Eastern Railway Magazine* for 1923, diagrams, plans, staff instruction books, newspaper cuttings, postcards and photographs of locomotives, letters and orders for sale of land to railway companies and papers relating to claims for compensation by owners of land through which the Eastern Counties Railway passed. Some of these books and magazines form part of a miscellaneous collection of publications, bequeathed to the record office by A C Sandwell.

Another item of interest is an interview, in the Essex Sound Archive, made in 1992 with Jack Rayner who was born in 1927, where he recalls visiting his grandfather's signal box and his father's and his own work on the railways.

There is also a large amount of material from the Great Yarmouth Port and Haven Commission held amongst the Great Yarmouth Borough Archives at the Norfolk Record Office. These include Acts of Parliament, railway bills and legal actions, plans and petitions referring to railway lines running out of Yarmouth.

The Suffolk offices all have some railway material, especially plans.

Private, estate and business records also include may relevant records. An interesting set of items are the business records at Ipswich Record Office for R Garrett Ltd, engineers, who ran an agricultural machinery company adjoining Leiston railway station. These include railway accounts and descriptions and sketches of equipment supplied to railway companies. Also at Ipswich Record Office, amongst private papers in the Rous Family Archives, are a bundle of papers that include a prospectus for the Ipswich and Yarmouth Coast Railway 1840–1852, with map.

It is possible to find railway memorabilia and copies of newspaper reports, especially relating to accidents and deaths, in all local archives. Mention of railways can also occur in unrelated news items. When Robert Seaman died in 1874, for instance, his obituary in the *Norfolk Chronicle* remarked that:

> …the immediate cause of death was an attack of bronchitis, the result of a cold caught a fortnight previous at the railway station in Yarmouth, while waiting for a train.

Census returns and birth, marriage and death certificates are extremely good for identifying occupations associated with railway work. The addresses on these and in trade directories can also reveal whether someone was living close to a railway works or line.

12.2 Bringing it to Life

There are a great many railway and transport heritage centres and publications illustrating the history and impact of the railways. The main centre for information and historical background is the National Railway Museum in York. This has an excellent library of railway publications and a collection of over a million photographs of trains, stations and railway personnel dating from the 1850s.

A selection of photographs from the Railway Museum collection can be viewed at the Science and Society Picture Library www.scienceandsociety.co.uk

The Red Wheel scheme is a major new initiative administered by the Transport Trust, celebrating Britain's transport legacy. It marks sites of special historic interest with a Red Wheel plaque carrying links to a dedicated website setting out the site's history and importance. Railway sites included for Cambridgeshire are Cambridge railway station, the Great Chesterford and Newmarket railway level crossing cottage and the Whitemoor marshalling yard at March, once the largest in Britain and the second largest in Europe. Essex sites featured include Maldon East station and goods shed, Roydon station and the narrow gauge railway at Gunpowder Mills. Among the Norfolk sites represented are the Outwell goods office for the Wisbech and Outwell Tramway, whilst Suffolk sites include Bury St Edmunds, Needham and Stowmarket stations.

A designated website for the Red Wheel scheme is in progress. In the meantime information can be found at the information page www.transporttrust.com/10078.html on the Transport Trust website www.transporttrust.com

The East Anglia Railway Museum at Chappel Station, just outside Colchester, is a working museum dedicated to preserving railway history. As well as displays of railway stock and memorabilia, and the opportunity to ride on trains, there are steam railway experience courses

Other places of interest include Soham, where a plaque commemorates engine driver Ben Gimbert, fireman James Nightall and signalman Frank Bridges, who saved Soham from disaster when their ammunition train caught fire as it passed through the town in July 1944. Bridges and Nightall were killed and all three were awarded the George Cross.

When the Great Eastern railway express was derailed at Witham in Essex in 1905, killing eleven people, it was widely reported in national and local newspapers. Some photographs can also be found at Essex Record Office.

Colne Valley Railway at Castle Hedingham station, near Halstead in Essex, has a running line, steam locomotives, reconstructed station, signal box, railway yard and miniature railway.

The North Norfolk Railway at Sheringham runs a 10.5 mile round trip by steam train through north Norfolk and has a museum of the railway's history.

The Mid Suffolk Light Railway Museum at Wetheringsett has interesting displays on this aspect of railway history.

Saxmundham Museum includes a scale model of Saxmundham railway station as it was in the 1930s, with working trains.

In Norfolk, the railway station at Wymondham was built in 1845 on the Norwich to Ely line. Still a working railway line, the station has been restored, and its buildings house a railway museum. It regularly wins awards for 'best kept railway station' and has also featured in several films and television shows.

Bressingham Steam Museum in Norfolk has one of world's finest collections of British and Continental locomotives, including the *Royal Scot*.

The collection of broadsheets held by the Norfolk Heritage Centre includes a series relating to railways dating from the 1840s. These include notices of surveys, and public meetings about proposed lines to accidents. My own personal favourite is a challenge sent to the directors of the Eastern Counties Railway Company from George Hoy of London in 1856. In this he claims his old donkey could beat their business trains for speed, and is illustrated with a donkey racing a train. Some of the more poignant are the epithet and memorial to Peter Fagan and Edward Garrard, two enginemen killed while on duty in 1860, and the railway disaster in 1874 when the mail train from Great Yarmouth ran into the Express Train from Norwich. Many of these images can be seen via the Norfolk Sources website.

The East Anglian Film Archive at the Archives Centre in Norwich has a large number of films about the history of transport construction and services. Topics include railways, buses, trams, cars, lorries, farm vehicles and bicycles. It is possible to view scenes about the history of the railway network in the region; amateur enthusiasts own films of local branch lines in the 1950s and 60s and a British Transport Film, on the electrification of the London to Southend railway line, amongst others.

Chapter 13

URBANIZATION AND HOUSING

The spread of urbanization and the corresponding growth in housing may not be immediately apparent as a subject for family history research. Yet, it is intimately linked to our ancestors' experiences.

Until the mid-nineteenth century most of England's population still lived off the land. Whilst many timber-framed, brick, cob and stone houses built between the mid 1500s and the early 1800s still survive in villages, even the most simple of these were originally built for wealthier inhabitants. The majority of workers lived in single or two-roomed cottages, hovels and longhouses, most of which no longer exist. In general the materials used prior to the nineteenth century were local as only the wealthy could afford to transport stone from elsewhere, although finely cut pieces of masonry were recycled from old monasteries and abandoned churches.

Timber-framed houses were constructed well into the 1700s, especially at the lower end of the social scale, but locally produced brick gradually became more popular for both building and decorative work. In parts of East Anglia a variety of methods using clays and muds, interlaced with straw, remained popular until the nineteenth century. The process of pargetting was extremely popular in East Anglia, especially in parts of Suffolk and Essex. This was a process whereby a new facade was created by coating plaster over strips of wood fixed to the front of a house and then combing patterns into it. The use of horizontal wooden boards as a weatherproof cover, often with mathematical tiles, later added on the outside to imitate bricks, was another popular local style in this region. At the bottom of the social scale were the cottagers, landless labourers and domestic servants who, by the eighteenth century, made up half the population of England. Despite improved living conditions and educational opportunities for some, most still lived in very basic accommodation.

Rural housing in Short Stone Lane in Cley-next-the-Sea in the early 1900s.

As huge advances in manufacturing technologies particularly in textiles and metal products fuelled the industrial revolution, more and more people moved out of the countryside in search of employment, leading to enormous changes in society and people's surroundings.

The population in England and Wales grew from 9 million in 1801 to over 30 million in 1901. Although rural areas like much of Suffolk continued to develop at a pre-industrial pace, large towns grew into great cities and smaller towns into larger ones. Cities like Cambridge, Colchester and Norwich grew rapidly, while ports, industrial towns and fashionable resorts like Cromer, Southwold and Clacton-on-Sea expanded dramatically, with rows of terraces springing up in response to the demands of a growing population. In Essex, for instance, by 1991 over 90 per cent of the county's population lived in an urban area compared with 16 per cent in 1831. Urbanization, therefore, had a major impact on lifestyle, work opportunities and even the health and leisure of numerous people.

From the eighteenth century onwards housing for the majority of people started to undergo dramatic changes as tighter regulations, increased wealth and a booming population resulted in an increasing standardization of styles. This was partially because of the haste to erect cheap housing in response to growing demand and partially because improved road networks and new canals meant building materials such as bricks could be transported cheaply instead of being made locally. All major cities and large towns in England were noted for their squalor and overcrowding, a situation which did not change dramatically for several generations.

The transport revolution fundamentally changed the nature of large cities in the second half of the nineteenth century by making the separation of city centres and living quarters possible. Most new houses were urban terraces, divided into classes and regulated by legislation, with their facades influenced by the need to reduce fire risk. There were also the beginnings of the massive growth of smaller terraced housing, built for the working and lower middle classes, in cities and their suburbs, although thousands of these houses were sub-standard.

The position of the working classes gradually began to improve despite poverty, disease and uncertain employment. As a result, most could expect to live in a house with around four rooms by the time Queen Victoria died in 1901, rather than be crammed into one room as many had to when she came to the throne in 1837. Movements to provide housing on a substantial scale to replace slums began in the 1840s with the building funded by shares. Large

Norwich St Lawrence Court in 1916.

scale slum clearance, together with municipal housing provision, was further aided by the Housing of the Working Classes Act in 1890.

Although Norwich fell behind industrial centres in the north and Midlands it still had a population of over 100,000 by 1900. In the first part of the eighteenth century the city was dirty, overcrowded and unsanitary. Under pressure from the growing population and expanding industries, hamlets, which had been separate rural parishes, became subsumed by the spread of building. Houses for the middle classes were built in places like Thorpe Road in Thorpe Hamlet. This area was developed partially because it was close to the new railway station, enabling easy access to transport.

Another area dramatically affected was Stratford in Essex. What was a rural village on the edge of London at the beginning of the 1800s was radically transformed after the Eastern Counties railway line began operating through Stratford in 1839. The main works for the building of locomotives and carriages for the Great Eastern Railway opened a few years later on a seventy-eight acre site that became known as the 'Rail Lands', employing thousands of people. From the 1920s this was also used as a depot for repairs and maintenance.

Taking the parish of Heigham in Norfolk as an example, it is possible to track the spread of cities into the countryside. Originally, a separate parish on the edge of Norwich, Heigham was the site for the earliest terraced housing built for the working classes in the city. Much of the land in this area was owed by the Unthank family who sold it to developers who arranged the layout of the streets and sewers. The houses were erected from what is now the Vauxhall Street area, leading out from the old city boundary at Chapelfield Road. When comparing early maps such as Faden's with the later tithe map of 1839 and the first ordnance survey map from the 1880s, it is possible to see how the street plan follows some of the original field boundaries.

Marlborough Place terrace on Rupert Street was built in 1867 following the sale of large parts of the land in this area of Heigham by the Unthank family. Numbers 78 to 88 Rupert Street survived bomb damage in the Second World War and encapsulate the expansion of the city in the nineteenth century from its medieval core to the present day metropolis. These houses are now universally viewed as central Norwich. The deeds to number 86 Rupert Street in Norwich demonstrate how restrictions on the design and look of properties were commonly imposed when the land was sold for development. Every dwelling house was to be:

...faced in the front with good white bricks...to be covered with good slates and have iron gutters in front and sides (except as to shop windows) have sash windows only and should be placed fronting the said streets called Rupert Street and Church Street in a straight line on the building line.

...no workshop privy or outbuilding should be allowed to front the said streets...the sides of every dwellinghouse should be coloured or as near as might be like the front.

...no frontispiece porch...should extend more than 18 inches from such building line and that every frontispiece porch or other similar projection should be made of wood or composition That no dwellinghouse should be less than 18 feet 3 in from the floor line to the top of the wall plate and that the floor line should not be less than 9 inches above the crown of the said streets.

Victorian terraced housing built on Marlborough Terrace, Rupert Street in 1867 to cater for the expanding population of Norwich.

The deeds go on to state that certain activities were also to be restricted, the amount the houses could be let for should not be less than £9, no building or erection should be more than two stories high and every gate was to open inwards.

The Edwardian period saw the various attempts to solve the problem of working-class housing. Competitions and exhibitions were held with the aim of producing cheaper houses so slums could be cleared. Despite their egalitarian principles most of these became middle-class centres and had little impact on getting rid of city slums. Nevertheless, the idea grew and led to the later building of council houses and new towns.

The spread of a cheap suburban rail network meant middle class families could live further out of town on cheaper land which, in turn, meant they could afford a bigger house with a garden, most typified by the semi-detached house. Working class people could escape the worst areas of towns by tram and bicycle and some were able to afford to buy their own terraced house, with the very fortunate having their own privy. An example of this would be Mildmay Road in Romford, Essex, which has a mix of terraced and semi-detached houses, built outside the original village with easy access to a suburban railway line, the underground and bus services.

The inter-war years was the period in which housing began to reap the benefits of previous generations' efforts to redress the balance of the nation's wealth. Schemes such as 'Homes Fit for Heroes', which promised homes and jobs in reward for the sacrifices made during the First World War, were the first attempts at a national programme of local authority housing, with council estates such as Mile Cross in Norwich built in the 1920s.

The slum clearances of the 1930s, followed by the destruction caused by bombing attacks during the Second World War enabled a new vision of how urban areas could be reconstructed. New towns like Harlow, Chelmsford and Basildon in Essex and Peterborough in Cambridgeshire heralded a new era in town planning. These were built as part of a far reaching government plan to transfer people and industries out of Greater London. Every detail was planned before any brick was laid, with those built around existing towns chosen because they already had industries close to a railway, near a supply of labour and reasonably close to London. Chelmsford for example was chosen because of its well established electronics industry associated with Marconi.

13.1 Finding out More

Many of the general sources for discovering information about the housing of people who lived in urban areas from the late eighteenth century onwards, are those already discussed in the sections on property, and land ownership and tenancy.

Census returns, electoral registers and trade directories, among other sources, assist in tracking where people lived. Newspapers carried reports on new housing projects and many photographs and oral histories survive. Deeds, plans, ordnance survey maps, tithe and enclosure maps, photographs, city and borough engineers records and building control plans, illustrate how new developments grew up around existing buildings and on once green fields. As mentioned, in the introduction to this book, large numbers of these records can be found in local archives. Listings to specific places can be found in the various record office indexes and catalogues, both locally and online. The A2A website again proves invaluable in tracking down many of these.

There are also a variety of other records, such as rate books, which include details of owners and occupiers of properties. Again, details of these can be found in all local archives.

13.2 Bringing it to Life

Many of the regions' museums and heritage centres have displays and exhibitions illustrating population and housing changes.

Open to the public in Lavenham, Suffolk, is the Little Hall on the market place, built in the 1390s. Originally built as a family house and workplace, it was divided in the eighteenth century into tenements and provided homes for six families for almost 200 years.

The Rows in Great Yarmouth was a medieval network of tiny courtyards and narrow alleys, just two feet wide in places. Badly damaged during a bombing raid in 1942, only a small section survives. There were originally 145 rows, totalling around seven miles, all built at right angles to the sea, and therefore ventilated by onshore breezes.

New towns such as Harlow in Essex demonstrate a unique period in housing provision. The museum in Harlow has a copy of the original master plan for the new town.

A Great Yarmouth row in 1930.

Chapter 14

RELIGION

Religion played a major role in our ancestors' lives, both spiritually and in the practical role religious organizations have had in day-to-day life. Wherever your ancestors were from and whether they were religious or not, it is impossible to research your ancestry to any great extent without using church records, in particular, parish registers. This is because Christianity underpins our legal and political system.

The parish was responsible for both civil and ecclesiastical (church) administration until the mid-1800s. The church building was originally used for both religious observance and as a meeting place to conduct practical business. The parish church has therefore been at the heart of every community, with many standing in the same place for nearly a thousand years.

Parish responsibilities included amongst other things: moral supervision by the parish priest and his officers, law enforcement by the parish constable, provision for the poor, highway maintenance and management of commons and open fields. This wide spectrum of duties in turn created countless records. Church of England records of all kinds are therefore a crucial resource, particularly before the beginning of civil registration (1837) and the first census returns to include names (1841). Church records also include probate records from before the reformation of the sixteenth century as the church was responsible for their administration.

Nonconformists still appear in Church of England parish registers. This is partially because the Hardwicke Act of 1754 stated that everyone, except Quakers and Jews, must marry in a church, something which did not change until civil registration was introduced in 1837. Religious intolerance and restrictions on worship often led Nonconformists to use the Church of

Binham Priory in Norfolk, founded in the eleventh century and still used as a church today.

England for baptisms and burials, especially if their employer was a church member.

Practical reasons may have also been a factor. Burial registers, for instance, contain Nonconformist entries where there was no alternative burial ground. An alternative reason may have been because one of the criteria for claiming poor relief was to have been born in a parish. Therefore, some parents might have their children baptized within the Church as a means of establishing a parish of settlement.

Occasionally parents had their children baptized in more than one church. An example is Charles and Maria Boyd who had children baptized in both the Anglican church and the Church Gate Street Presbyterian Church in Bury St Edmunds in Suffolk in the early 1800s.

Roman Catholics in particular may have paid lip service to religious conformity as they were excluded from certain areas of public life before the Catholic Emancipation Act of 1829. Such discrimination probably lies behind why the children of Knipe and Jane Gobbet are included in the registers of both the Anglican church in Tacolneston and the Norwich Catholic church in the 1760s. Although his wife was baptized a Roman Catholic Knipe was a prominent local wine merchant, JP, alderman, sheriff, mayor and lieutenant colonel of the West Norfolk Militia.

A C Edwards, in his history of Essex, illustrates the story of religious change in the sixteenth century through the account books of parishes in the Great Dunmow area. These show the destruction of stone altars and the rood screen, and the covering of religious paintings in whitewash during the reign of Edward VI. When Mary Tudor became queen the churchwardens tried to restore their church to its former state by buying a Latin service book and reintroducing processional banners. As soon as Mary died, the church at Great Dunmow removed all Catholic trappings.

14.1 Nonconformists

The first Protestant Nonconformist congregations appeared in the second half of the seventeenth century and include Presbyterians, Baptists, Methodists, Independents and Quakers. Extreme Protestants or 'Puritans' as they became known, wanted a 'purer' form of worship and objected to anything reminiscent of the Church of Rome. They were so harshly suppressed that many emigrated to America in the early seventeenth century. When the *Mayflower* sailed from Plymouth in 1620 on its historic voyage, more than half the 102 pilgrims came from East Anglia. Amongst those from Essex was the governor of the ship, Christopher Martin of Billericay.

By the reign of Charles I, the Church of England was deeply divided. When the Civil War broke out in 1642, most Puritans supported the Parliamentarian side. With the Restoration of Charles II in 1660, the Anglican bishops and other clergy were restored. Parliament then passed laws making it impossible for anyone to be a Member of Parliament, town councillor or Army officer unless they took communion in the Anglican Church. Most Puritans then left the Church, becoming Nonconformists because they would not conform to Anglican teaching. By the eighteenth century, the laws preventing Nonconformists holding public office had been either repealed or fallen into disuse.

14.2 Baptists

Baptists have a complex history dating back to the Reformation. Traditionally, they believe all authority derives from the bible. Common aspects include the baptism of adults rather than children, baptism via full immersion, the independence of local churches and religious revivals. As with many Nonconformist groups they formed wide ranging geographical links with other congregations. Examples can be seen in the Norwich St Mary Baptist registers for 1791 where the burial of 22 year old Mary Barber of St Andrew's in Norwich is recorded as having taken place in 1789 in the 'Protestant Dissenters Burying-Ground, in Wisbech Isle of Ely'. Another person buried elsewhere was 2 year old Julia Ninham of St Edmunds Norwich, who was buried in the 'Protestant Dissenters Burying-Ground in St Margaret's' in 1856.

14.3 Methodists

Methodism's promotion of sober living, hard work and good deeds, as the means to a better afterlife, was extremely appealing, especially amongst the working classes. As with all other denominations some areas of the region have a stronger presence than others, with the Fenland area of Cambridgeshire and west Norfolk having a particularly long association. Methodism also had an impact on the social reform movements and the development of trade unionism across the country, with people like the agricultural reformer George Edwards being members of the church. Over time, the religion divided into a number of smaller groups such as the Primitive Methodists and New Connexion.

14.4 Presbyterians, Separatists, Independents and Congregationalists

The history of Presbyterians, Congregationalists and Unitarians is frequently intertwined. Congregationalists, or Independents, did not agree with state interference with religion. Some who had a particular interest in science or reason became involved with the Unitarian movement in the eighteenth and nineteenth centuries. Out of this came the United Reform Church of the late twentieth century

Robert Browne was the first known leader of the Separatists and founder of Congregationalism. He was an Anglican preacher and pastor in Cambridgeshire who became unhappy with certain aspects of how the Church of England was run. He began by establishing a fellowship of like minded thinkers in Norwich, but was forced into exile in Holland. When he returned to England in 1584, he was imprisoned and excommunicated.

Stansted Mountfitchet Congregational Church around 1906.

Following a form of reconciliation with the established Church he became a teacher in Northamptonshire.

The Separatists were more radical than the Presbyterians, dissociating themselves from the Church of England and holding that membership of the Church was a privilege not a right. They held illegal assemblies based on Browne's teachings. In the early seventeenth century the Separatist movement adopted the name 'Independent' and began to found chapels. They gained strength in the Civil War as Oliver Cromwell was an Independent. One of the earliest Presbyterian chapels in East Anglia was the Old Meeting House in Colegate, Norwich, which was built in 1693.

By the early nineteenth century most Independents began to call themselves 'Congregationalists' as their focus had always been the autonomy of local fellowships or congregations. They formed a Union in 1832 and most chapels merged with the Presbyterians in 1972 to form the United Reform Church.

Again, the willingness of Nonconformist groups to travel to a church or chapel of their denomination can be seen in the Bungay Independent church registers which record many people from nearby parishes in both Suffolk and Norfolk.

14.5 The Society of Friends (Quakers)

Formed under George Fox in the 1640s, the Society of Friends, more commonly known as Quakers were always Nonconformist. Their teachings spread across East Anglia, especially in parts of north Essex, after George Fox visited Halstead in 1657. Prominent East Anglian Quakers, such as Elizabeth Fry and the Gurney and Sewell families, were social reformers who combined a social conscience with building banking and business dynasties.

Elizabeth Fry was born into the Gurney family of Norfolk. Her father Joseph was one of founders of Gurney's Bank, which later became Barclays. Motivated by the preaching of American Quaker, William Savery, Elizabeth became involved with working with the poor, sick and prisoners. Following her marriage to Joseph Fry and a move to London she became more actively involved in working to reform the prison system, particularly for women in Newgate. Elizabeth Fry's Essex born brother-in-law, Thomas Fowell Buxton was elected as Member of Parliament for Weymouth, and used his position to support her work and campaign for the abolition of slavery.

14.6 Roman Catholics

Roman Catholics had to wait longer than Nonconformists to be allowed to worship freely and hold public office. Despite their suppression and the dominance of the Anglican Church, there are some areas which had a strong Catholic presence in the region. These are more likely to be in areas where local landowners, like the Duke of Norfolk, were Catholic.

One example of the difficulties in tracking down such records can be seen with the Otley family from the Hengrave area of Suffolk. William and Beatrice Otley were both baptized and married in the Church of England. Following the employment of William as a gamekeeper by the Duke of Norfolk, and their subsequent relocation from Suffolk to Arundel in Sussex in the 1820s, some of their children were baptized in a Catholic chapel there. Although several children are recorded on subsequent census returns as being born in Suffolk, no baptisms for them have been found. Neither is there any evidence of whether William and Beatrice were brought up Catholic despite being baptized in the Anglican church, or if they converted, perhaps because of who their employer was.

14.7 Jews

Jewish settlers first arrived in England after the Norman Conquest from Rouen in Normandy. Expelled in 1290 under Edward I, the ban on Jewish settlement was not lifted until 1655, when Oliver Cromwell responded to an appeal by Dutch Jews. Small communities existed in East Anglia in places like Bury St Edmunds, Ipswich and Norwich. This can be seen in the *1851 Census of Religious Worship* which recorded only two synagogues in Yarmouth and Norwich, with congregations of less than thirty. In 1898 *The Jewish Yearbook* put the number of Jews in the City of Norwich at fifty. By the 1930s the city's community had grown to 130, and to 150 by 1945.

There are still small communities across the region. An extra influx occurred in Soham, Isleham and Fordham in Cambridgeshire during the Second World War when the pupils from the Jews' Free Central School in East London were evacuated to the area.

14.8 Finding out More

With so many types of records which could be found under the heading 'religion' it is best to offer some general guidance and a few examples regarding the main categories.

The vast majority of Church of England records, at least to around 1900, are held in local archives. Most are kept in the county record office to which the parish belongs. However, as mentioned in the introduction to this book, it is possible for records from one county to be stored in another county because they were the responsibility of a particular church authority.

There are an increasing number of indexes and transcripts available both in record offices and family history societies. The most comprehensive collections in the region are those at Cambridge and Huntingdon record offices.

Finding Nonconformist records can be more problematic. Because of persecution, hostility and intolerance, many Nonconformists either did not keep records, or they have not survived. There were also not the same obligations upon Nonconformists to record information as there was for the Church of England. Nevertheless, there are still many collections in local record offices.

A large number of Nonconformist records were collected by the government from 1837 and are now held at The National Archives (TNA). These can be accessed in the series RG 4 and RG 8. Copies of most of the registers deposited at TNA can also be found on film in local record offices and some family history societies. Lists of these can be found with those for local Nonconformist records. They can also be accessed online for a fee at www.thegenealogist.co.uk

Some Nonconformist churches and chapels made copies of the registers which they sent to the Registrar General for their own use, whilst others never handed theirs in. These local registers were often later deposited in county record offices, although others may still be with the local minister.

Some listings to Nonconformist records held locally, can be found on the A2A website and record offices' own online catalogues. However, these are not always as complete as those for Church of England registers so it is worth checking directly with archive staff.

Where they do exist, Nonconformist registers can often include far more information than those of the Church of England registers. The baptism of James Birt, in the registers for the Old Buckenham Methodist circuit in 1835, includes his date of birth as well as baptism, where he was born, his mother's maiden name and the signature of his parents. Those who compiled registers for the Congregationalist, Presbyterian and Independents across the region seem to be particularly fond of recording the occupation of the father, whilst some include genealogical information about other family members.

As already mentioned, Nonconformists can still appear in the baptismal, marriage and burial registers of the Anglican church. Details can also be found in other Anglican records. An Act in 1695 required incumbents to keep lists of 'dissenter' births; this meant children not baptized in the Church. Although this was largely ignored, some clergy did note baptisms of 'Anabaptists'. This technically referred to the adult baptisms of those who decided to be accepted into the Anglican Church, but was also used as a generic term for all Nonconformists.

The annual register bills, which were copies of every baptism, marriage and burial sent to the Archdeacon or Bishops, were meant to include the number of 'papists' or 'recusants' in a parish. Again, not all clergy filled in this information, but where they did, the details can range from a simple statement such as 'none' or a set of numbers, to the inclusion of individuals' names and personal comments on local Nonconformists, especially those who refused to pay tithes to the Church of England.

A variety of records can be found for the Separatist, Congregationalist and Independent congregations across the region. Amongst these are records held at Norfolk Record Office from the Great Yarmouth Middlegate Congregational Church Books which date from 1643 to 1760.

Records relating to Roman Catholics can be especially difficult to find before restrictions on Catholic worship were lifted in the nineteenth century. Amongst the records held in the Norfolk Record Office are a 'Text of address [for] Norfolk Catholic Families 1570 to 1780', with an alphabetical list of Norfolk Catholics 1664–1669 and an index of Catholics named in the 'Return of Papists' for 1767, which listed 'recusants'. Some Roman Catholic records in the region have been transcribed, including the baptismal registers for Norwich for 1758 to 1823. This also includes biographical notes on some prominent families.

Some general records dating from the 1870s relating to the Catholic church in Beccles, Suffolk, can also be found at the Norfolk Record Office in the 'Personal and Religious Papers of the Kenyon Family of Gillingham Hall'. These are mainly administrative and financial, but include items such as the 'Society for relief of discharged Catholic prisoners, 1877–1885'. A variety of papers and correspondence relating to Catholicism can also be found in several collections at Cambridge University Library.

With regards to Methodist records there are some quite large collections in local record offices. The Thetford Methodist Circuit for example has a series of records deposited at Norfolk Record Office. Their Circuit Schedules include the names and numbers of preachers in each circuit; how many people belonged to the circuit and sums of money collected for various reasons such as the 'Worn-out ministers and Widows' Fund'.

Preaching plans, lists of local preachers, circuit books, schedules, quarter meeting and local preachers' minutes include the names and locations of local preachers, including transfers between different circuits, and detailed information about the activities of preachers and members of their congregation.

Methodism had a strong presence in the west of the Norfolk, with many links between circuits serving parishes in the Methwold, Northwold and Upwell area and those parishes in circuits just over the Suffolk and Cambridgeshire borders. It is, therefore, common to find people from these areas listed in the records of adjoining counties.

Preachers also travelled long distances and maintained connections across the world. When Clement Reeve, a Wesleyan preacher for Northwold, in the Thetford circuit, left for Tasmania in 1855 his fares were paid by a prominent settler there. When he left the circuit, schedules record the word 'Australia' next to his name in a list of people moving to other circuits and the minutes include a tribute to him.

Details on how the ministry was organized and disagreements between members are also revealed in these minutes. Some examples are: Mr Griffin and J Kirchen were reported as having left the Methwold circuit in 1846, that Messers Cock and Webb visited Foulden in March 1848 but could not obtain a house to preach in and there was a charge by Brother Gathercole against Brother John Cock junior, in March 1852, 'for the use of very strong & objectionable language in reference to a sermon preached at Brandon by Br G on a recent occasion'. In June it was reported that the case had been settled amicably.

The Countess Huntingdon, Selina Hastings (1707–91), was the founder of the Calvinistic Methodist sect, the 'Countess of Huntingdon Connexion'. She opened private chapels attached to her residences, which she was allowed to do as a peeress of the realm. When they became a source of contention with local Anglican clergy, she ceded from the Church of England in 1781. A few records and transcripts can be found locally, mostly at Cambridgeshire Record Office, with one set of registers on film in the Norfolk office.

The Cambridgeshire Record Offices all have printed copies of an index to all Cambridgeshire and Huntingdonshire entries in Dr Williams' Library, London, which acted as a registry for Baptists, Independents and Presbyterians between

The Friends' Meeting House in Gildengate, Norwich.

1742 and 1837. This index covers births from 1754 to 1837 and births and baptisms from 1812 to 1837.

Quakers were often fined, imprisoned or transported for refusing to take oaths, serve in the armed forces, attend Anglican Church services, or pay tithes to parish clergymen. The Quaker Act of 1662 specifically penalized anyone refusing to take an oath and for more than five Quakers meeting for worship. As a result references can be found in court records and Anglican church records.

Some parish registers also include reference to Quakers, sometimes specifically to their refusing to pay tithes to the Anglican Church. The Quaker Family History Society has produced a large number of indexes and transcripts to records and registers, including those for East Anglia.

A reflection of the strong presence of Dutch and Walloon communities in the region is evidenced by the churches they had in Norwich. The Dutch used Blackfriar's Hall, whilst the Walloons took over the church of St Mary the Less in 1637 for their services in French until 1832. The Dutch registers can be found in the British Library and the Guildhall Library, whilst the Walloon registers are in The National Archives. However, there are various published transcripts, of which the record office and family history society have copies.

Essex, Cambridgeshire and Norfolk all had Huguenot settlements in Colchester, the Fenland area of Thorney Abbey, and Norwich. Surviving registers have been transcribed by the Huguenot Society and copies can be found in local archives, local studies libraries and family history societies.

There are few Jewish records held locally, but some local archives have copies of the *Jewish Yearbook*, which includes some genealogical information. *Tracing Jewish Ancestors* by Rosemary Wenzenul (Pen & Sword Family History, 2008) provides a thorough guide to finding and using records relating to Jewish ancestry.

Local antiquarian, Walter Rye, compiled a transcript to the Monumental Inscriptions in the Jewish Cemetery, Great Yarmouth, which can be accessed at the Norfolk Record Office.

The Suffolk Record Offices have copies of an article on the Jewish community in Ipswich published in the *Suffolk Institute of Archaeology (Vol. XL, 2004)* by Robert Halliday and Bernard Susser. This describes the history of Jews in the town, including some genealogical details of local Jewish families.

When the national census returns were introduced from 1801, it inspired some local clergymen to compile their own religious census, which includes details about the religion of parishioners. This can be found amongst local parish records.

Records which reveal the numbers of people associated with different religious denominations include the 1851 census of *Accommodation and Attendance at Worship* generally referred to as the Religious Census. Although its purpose was statistical, it provided a comprehensive listing of English denominations and their whereabouts as well as statistical data on attendance. Some of the reports for each county have been republished separately, and copies can be found in local record offices and local studies libraries.

Trade Directories, which were published from the late eighteenth century onwards, list local churches and chapels as well as other significant religious houses.

Wills can often reveal individual's religious leanings, either through a request that they be buried in a particular place or bequests to particular churches or chapels. When Mary Sutton of Norwich wrote her will in 1757, for instance, she left £10 to the deacons and one guinea to the minister of the independent congregation. The phrasing used in wills written before the introduction of a civil probate system in 1858, often provides an indication of someone's religion. For example, when Philip Pank of Costessey in Norfolk left a will in 1790 it began with 'In the name of the Holy Trinity', thereby making his Catholicism explicit. In contrast if the executor of a will before 1858 was a Quaker they would be recorded as making an affirmation rather than taking the oath to the crown.

As mentioned, in the section on court records, Nonconformist ministers had to be licensed until the early nineteenth century. One example is the certificate of appointment in 1807 amongst the Norfolk Quarter Sessions papers that states the 'Methodists of Beechamwell St Mary who worship in the house of William Smith, blacksmith, appoint John Clarke, carrier as Preacher'. Another is the application for licences for Protestant Dissenters' meeting houses at Shalford and Aythorpe Roding in 1726, held amongst the Essex Quarter Sessions.

14.9 Bringing it to Life

Although visiting churches, chapels, meeting houses, synagogues and so on may not be viewed as an essential part of family history research, such visits will provide context to your research. I am not going to suggest any one place to visit, simply because there is such a wealth of possible places.

What I believe really brings the past to life is to at least visit or obtain a picture of the local church in the parish where your ancestors lived. Churches provide a direct link to the past, both practically and visually, and their existence literally makes it possible to stand in your ancestors' footsteps. This is because even Nonconformists and non Christians would have had some dealings with the church authorities through the paying of rates, the proving of wills and the receipt of poor relief. They are also some of the few ancient buildings still standing today which are, for the most part, still used for the purpose for which they were built.

Gravestones in the churchyard of St Mary and St Botolph, Thorney Abbey, Cambridgeshire, provide evidence of a Huguenot colony that settled there at the request of Oliver Cromwell, after fleeing France in the aftermath of the St Bartholomew's Day massacre in 1572.

Several parts of Norwich City centre have links to the Jewish community. Synagogue Street off Mountergate is the only street with this name in England. A plaque marks the site of the synagogue built there in 1848, after which the street is named. One of the oldest standing houses in Norwich,

'Jurnets' or 'The Music House' on King Street, belonged to a Jewish family that lived in Norwich in the thirteenth century. Isaac Jurnet, who is believed to have been the wealthiest Jewish businessman in England at the time, was also the chief money lender to the abbot and monks of Westminster. The awe inspiring undercroft is, in my opinion, one of the best in the country.

There are a number of histories, both published and private, of local Nonconformist churches and chapels, Jewish and Roman Catholic communities, often including genealogical information on local people. Many of these can be found in the regions record offices and libraries.

Bury St Edmunds record office, for example, has copies of several articles on local Nonconformist churches and chapels, including *The History of Presbyterians in Bury St Edmunds* by J Duncan, which records the history of the Church Gate Street church, originally published in the *Journal of the Presbyterian Historical Society 12* (1960–63).

The Great Yarmouth and Norwich Congregational Church Books include a history of the church in Norfolk referring to 'our English Church in Rotterdam', and giving details of the how the church was run, church members in trouble, and the careers and movements of leading figures.

A transcript of the Wesleyan Methodist Records for the Ramsey circuit, held in the Huntingdon record office, includes a history of the Methodist movement in the area. This describes how John Wesley travelled by horse, boat and chaise to St Ives to preach when he was over 70 years of age. By 1784 a small group of followers were meeting at the house of Mrs Elizabeth Asplin. In 1793 St Ives was listed as a Methodist society at Conference and a minister was stationed there. Land on Flag Holt in Ramsey was acquired and a chapel and school built in 1831. From later reports the chapel was about 45 feet by 36 feet with pews, galleries on three sides and a pulpit, with the 1854 Gazetteer stating it seated 600. By the 1890s a larger church was needed and John Evison, a farmer and owner of a chemical manure works, acquired the site of the old workhouse in Ramsey High Street in 1888 for £200 and gave it to the church trustees.

Mention of Nonconformists frequently appears in contemporary accounts such as the history of the village of Wortham in Suffolk written by the rector, Richard Cobbold. For instance, he described how the Quaker, 'Old John Pretty' was converted and publicly baptized in the church when he was over 80 years old, whereas Mrs Osborn refused to have her children baptized on the basis that there was nothing in scripture to prove infants should be.

A forthcoming book by Keith Reeve of Caringbah in Australia entitled *Brothers in Methodism – Clement Reeve and the Cock Families of Northwold and*

Methwold in the mid-nineteenth Century traces the relationship between the author's great-grandfather, Clement Reeve, a local Methodist preacher, and two patrician Methodist families of Northwold and Methwold, including some genealogical data. One of the sources for this history was an unpublished account of the Cock family history deposited at the record office. Once published, copies will be available at the record office, the heritage centre and family history society.

Some early references from the 1820s and 1830s to Catholicism, especially in relation to the Catholic Emancipation Act can be found in the papers of the Gage family of Hengrave held at Bury St. Edmunds.

The Suffolk Record Office in Lowestoft has a collection of photographs relating to the Catholic communities in Beccles and Bungay and pilgrimages to Dunwich in the early twentieth century. These can be found in the North East Suffolk Photographic and Illustrative Archive.

14.10 Monumental Inscriptions

Gravestones can be extremely useful for identifying family relationships as well as supplying extra personal details. There have been various projects to record memorials in churches and churchyards since at least the nineteenth century such as those transcribed in 1883–85 under the care of the *National Society for Preserving the Memorials of the Dead*. Many of these are held at local record offices, family history societies or the relevant church or cemetery.

In Bury St Edmunds the monumental inscriptions for St Mary's were recorded in 1887 by the Reverend Haslewood. As some gravestones were subsequently moved and others are no longer legible, the copy at the Bury St Edmunds office includes details of many that can no longer be identified, such as the combined inscription to Benjamin Burlingham, son of George and Margaret, in 1825 and George, son of Benjamin and Priscilla Burlingham, in 1838.

The Women's Institute carried out many churchyard surveys across the country in the 1980s, with copies given to every participating church, local record offices and studies libraries. Norfolk was one of the counties that participated and around a third of the county was covered.

The three Cambridgeshire record offices have some good collections of graveyard surveys, including several Nonconformist churches and chapels. Another of the databases the Cambridgeshire family history society has put online is their index to Cambridgeshire burials, 1801–1837, including Nonconformist burial grounds.

Most local family history societies have an active programme of collecting and recording monumental inscriptions. Many donate copies to local record offices, but some can only be found through a society. Others, like mid Norfolk and Cambridgeshire also add theirs to the National Burial Index.

Essex family history society has been prolific in compiling church and churchyard surveys, with copies donated to the record office. The record office online catalogue includes the name indexes to some of these.

In Suffolk, online indexes can be found for the cemeteries of Beccles, Bungay, Halesworth, Kirkley, Lowestoft, Southwold, Wrentham and the Royal Naval Patrol at the Waveney District Council Cemetery Online.

www.waveney.gov.uk/Environment/Cemeteries/cemeteries_index.htm

The National Archive of Memorial Inscriptions (NAOMI) includes nearly 600 Norfolk burial grounds and churches. Searching the index is free, but there is a small fee for obtaining full details at: www.memorialinscriptions. org.uk

14.11 Cemetery Records

Cemetery records generally date from the mid-nineteenth century. The oldest cemetery in England is the Rosary Cemetery in Norwich, which was established in 1819 by Presbyterian Minister, Thomas Drummond, to provide a burial place for people of all denominations.

Overcrowding, and contamination of the water supply by waste matter from the city churchyards, were increasing health hazards. In Norwich, for instance, half of the city's water pumps were next to churches. In 1853, an act was passed enabling local authorities to administer their own cemeteries and most city churchyards were subsequently closed.

The overall design, landscaping, and architecture were of great importance. The horticultural journalist, John Claudius Loudon, who laid out the Cambridge General Cemetery, published an influential book in 1843 called *On the Laying Out, Planting and Managing of Cemeteries*. This contained very detailed practical advice such as sub-dividing small level sites with straight drives and walks, and using broad sweeps to ease the gradients on larger, hilly sites.

In order to cater for both Anglicans and Nonconformists equally, early cemeteries provided a pair of chapels each surrounded by their own areas of

The Rosary Cemetery, the oldest cemetery in England.

the cemetery. From the 1850s these chapels were frequently presented as a single symmetrical composite building, usually set either parallel to one another or end to end, and linked by a covered carriage entrance.

14.12 Finding out More

Some cemetery records are deposited in record offices. The majority of these are for cemeteries in cities and boroughs. Those not deposited are kept by the relevant local authorities. The nearest council office will have contact details.

As well as burial registers many collections of cemetery records include grave books which list everyone buried in a particular plot. These also record whether the plot was privately owned or not.

Cambridgeshire, Huntingdonshire and Wisbech Record Offices all have some records, indexes and transcripts to local cemeteries.

Essex Record Office also has some records for the county. Some Essex people will be buried at one of the London cemeteries. Again, some of these are still held by the relevant council office, whilst others will be held at one of the London archives.

In Norfolk, various cemetery records for Norwich, Great Yarmouth and King's Lynn are held at the record office with copies at the heritage centre. These include registers for the Rosary Cemetery mentioned above. The memorial inscriptions from 1819–1986, and burial registers from 1821–1837 for the Rosary have also been recorded and indexed and copies of these can be found at the family history society, record office and heritage centre.

The Suffolk offices have several sets of cemetery records; those for Woodbridge Cemetery, for example. Ipswich Record Office include various indexes and registers to the 1940s. The indexes, in themselves, are helpful as they give a name, residence, age, date of death and grave location. The 1885 burial entry for Frederick Robert Banyard gives his address and describes him as eight months old and the son of Thomas, a carpenter.

14.13 Bringing it to Life

Again, there are a great many cemeteries which are worth visiting whether or not you have ancestors buried there. If I had to pick just one then it's always worth visiting my 'home' cemetery – the Rosary in Norwich – to see the many fine gothic monuments.

Resources Directory

Archives, Libraries and Local Studies Centres

Cambridgeshire

Cambridgeshire Collection
Central Library, Lion Yard, Cambridge CB2 3QD
Tel: 0845 0455225
Local studies collection.

Cambridge Record Office – Cambridge
Shire Hall, Castle Hill. Cambridge CB3 0AP
Tel: 01223 717281
Email: county.records.cambridge@cambridgeshire.gov.uk
www.cambridgeshire.gov.uk/archives

Cambridge Record Office – Huntingdon
Grammar School Walk, Huntingdon PE29 3LF
Tel: 01480 375842
Email: county.records.hunts@cambridgeshire
www.cambridgeshire.gov.uk/archives
Due to move to new premises adjacent to the library in 2009.

Cambridge Record Office – Wisbech And Fenland Museum
Museum Square, Wisbech PE13 1ES
Tel: 01945 583817
Email: archives@wisbechmuseum.org.uk
www.wisbechmuseum.org.uk/collections_archives.htm

Cambridge University Library
West Road, Cambridge CB3 9DR
Tel: 01223 333000
www.lib.cam.ac.uk

Essex

Barking And Dagenham Local Studies Centre
Valence House Museum, Becontree Avenue, Dagenham DM8 3HT
www.barking-dagenham.gov.uk/4-valence/valence-menu.html
Local and family history resources for the Barking and Dagenham area
(Closed until May 2010).

Essex Place Names Project
c/o The Essex Record Office
Essex Society for Archaeology & History project recording place names and
exploring their origins.

Essex Record Office
Wharf Road, Chelmsford CM2 6YT
Tel: 01245 244644
Email: ero.enquiry@essexcc.gov.uk
www.essexcc.gov.uk/ero
Includes access to **Essex Sound and Video Archive**

Essex Record Office – Harlow Access Point
Museum of Harlow, Muskham Road, off First Avenue, Harlow CM20 2LF
Tel: 01279 454959
Email: ero.enquiry@essexcc.gov.uk

Essex Record Office – Saffron Walden Access Point
Saffron Walden Library.
2 King Street, Saffron Walden CB10 1ES
Tel: 01799 523178
Email: ero.saffronwalden@essexcc.gov.uk

Norfolk

King's Lynn Borough Archives
The Old Gaol House, Saturday Market Place, King's Lynn PE30 5DQ
Tel: 01553 774297
Email: norfrec@norfolk.gov.uk
Archives and museum charting the history of crime and punishment over three centuries.
Contact for museum: gaolhouse@west-norfolk.gov.uk

Norfolk Heritage Centre
2nd Floor, Norfolk and Norwich Millennium Library, The Forum, Millennium Plain, Norwich NR2 1AW
Tel: 01603 774740
Email: norfolk.studies.lib@norfolk.gov.uk
www.norfolk.gov.uk/heritagecentre

Norfolk Record Office
The Archive Centre, County Hall, Martineau Lane, Norwich NR1 2DQ
Tel: 01603 222599
Email: Norfrec@norfolk.gov.uk
www.archives.norfolk.gov.uk
Also the home of the **East Anglian Film Archive**
Tel: 01603 592664
www.uea.ac.uk/eafa

True's Yard, King's Lynn
North Street, King's Lynn PE30 1QW
Tel: 01553 770479
Email: trues.yard@virgin.net
www.welcome.to/truesyard
Fishing heritage museum including local and family history resources.

Suffolk

Suffolk Record Office – Bury St Edmunds
77 Raingate Street, Bury St. Edmunds IP33 2AR
Tel: 01284 352352

Email: bury.ro@libher.suffolkcc.gov.uk
www.suffolk.gov.uk/SRO

Suffolk Record Office – Ipswich
Gatacre Road. Ipswich IP1 2LQ
Tel: 01473 584541
Email: ipswich.ro@libher.suffolkcc.gov.uk
www.suffolk.gov.uk/SRO
Also responsible for coordinating the **Suffolk Voices** oral history project.

Suffolk Record Office – Lowestoft
Central Library, Clapham Road South. Lowestoft NR33 1DR
Tel: 01502 405357
Email: lowestoft.ro@libher.suffolkcc.gov.uk
www.suffolk.gov.uk/SRO

Woodbridge Library
Woodbridge Library Manager, Woodbridge IP12 1DT
Tel: 01394 625095
Email: help@suffolklibraries.co.uk
Local history material for the Woodbridge area.

Other Archives

British Library
St Pancras, 96 Euston road, London NW1 2DB
Tel: 020 7412 7676
Email: reader-services-enquiries@bl.uk
www.bl.uk

British Library Newspapers
Colindale Avenue, London NW9 5HE
Tel: 020 7412 7353
Email: newspapers@bl.uk
www.bl.uk

Guildhall Library, London
Aldermanbury, London EC2P 2EJ
Tel: 020 7332 1862

Email: manuscripts.guildhall@cityoflondon.gov.uk
www.cityoflondon.gov.uk/guildhalllibrary

London Metropolitan Archives
40 Northampton Road, London EC1R OHB
Tel 020 7332 3820
Email: ask.lma@cityoflondon.gov.uk
www.cityoflondon.gov.uk/lma

Probate Principal Registry
First Avenue house, 42–49 High Holborn, London WC1V 6NP
www.hmcourts-service.gov.uk

Probate Service
Probate Sub Registry, 1st Floor, Castle Chambers, Clifford Street, York YO1 9RG
Tel: 01904 666777

The National Archives
Kew, Richmond, Surrey TW9 4DU
Tel: 020 8876 3444
Contact: www.nationalarchives.gov.uk/contact/form
www.nationalarchives.gov.uk

Web Resources

Cambridgeshire
www.cambridgeshire.gov.uk/leisure/archives/online Online displays of archives from Cambridge Record Office.
www.ccan.co.uk Cambridgeshire Community Archive Network (CCAN). Photographs, oral and written reminiscences and video recordings from fifty local communities. Tel: 01223 712009. Email: ccan@cambridgeshiregov.uk
www.cfhs.org.uk/Search.html Online databases produced by Cambridgeshire Family History Society include baptisms, marriage, burials, poor law and military records.
www.cambridgeshire.gov.uk/community/bmd/Camdex Indexes to births, marriages and deaths from Cambridgeshire registry office indexes.

Essex

www.foxearth.org.uk/index.html Foxearth and District Local History Society. Research materials for the area around Borley, Foxearth, Liston and Pentlow in Essex and Suffolk.

www.essex.police.uk/museum/research.htm Essex Police Museum. Database listing over 3,000 officers who served between 1840 and 1930.

www.putmans.co.uk/oldwaltonindex.htm Photographs of Walton-in-the-Naze from the mid-nineteenth century to the present.

www.hulford.co.uk/years.html Essex Witch Trials. Listing 730 people accused of being, or consorting with, witches.

Norfolk

www.noah.norfolk.gov.uk Norfolk Online Access to Heritage (NOAH). Indexes to newspapers and library, museum and record office catalogues.

norlink.norfolk.gov.uk/02_Catalogue/02_001_Search.aspx?searchType=97 Picture Norfolk. A photographic collection from local archives including the Regimental Museum – can also be accessed via the NOAH site.

www.norfolksources.norfolk.gov.uk Norfolk Sources. Images of archival material including broadsides, trade directories and probate records.

www.genealogy.doun.org/transcriptions/index.php Norfolk Transcription Archive. Transcripts of Norfolk parish registers.

www.poppyland.co.uk/index.php?s=GRESACT Poppyland Publishing. Includes additional material relating to Gressenhall workhouse.

www.norfolkpubs.co.uk/utility/norfolk.htm List of Norfolk pubs including historical information.

www.historic-maps.norfolk.gov.uk/Emap/EMapExplorer.asp Norfolk E Map Explorer. Digitized enclosure, tithe, ordnance survey and aerial maps.

www.fadensmapofnorfolk.co.uk Digital redrawing of Faden's 1797 map of Norfolk.

www.norfarchtrust.org.uk Norfolk Archaeological Trust. Information on the Roman site of Caistor St Edmund's and many other sites of interest in the county.

www.norfolkmills.co.uk Norfolk Mills. List of local mills with historical information.

www.norfolkheritage.org.uk/default.asp Norfolk Heritage. Local history research material from the villages of Breckles, Happisburgh, Harleston, Mulbarton and Reepham.

Suffolk

www.senseofplacesuffolk.co.uk/index.html East of England Sense of Place Suffolk (EESOP Suffolk). Images from archives, local studies, museums and archaeology collections.

www.pdmhs.com Peak District Mines Historical Society. List of flint and chalk mines in Suffolk in 1896.

www.suffolkmills.org.uk Suffolk Mills.

www.waveney.gov.uk/Environment/Cemeteries/cemeteries_index.htm Indexes to the cemeteries of Beccles, Bungay, Halesworth, Kirkley, Lowestoft, Southwold, Wrentham and the Royal Naval Patrol.

General Web Resources

www.nationalarchives.gov.uk/nra The National Register of Archives. Includes nationwide lists of business records.

www.nationalarchives.gov.uk/a2a Access to Archives (A2A). References to sources in archives across the country.

www.archiveshub.ac.uk Archives Hub. Information on archive collections in UK universities and colleges.

www.genuki.org.uk GENUKI. Countrywide links relating to family and local history.

www.familia.org.uk FAMILIA. Guide to genealogical resources in libraries.

www.cyndislist.com Cyndi's List of Genealogy Sites. Links and useful information worldwide.

www.familyhistoryonline.net Federation of Family History Societies databases, including the National Burial Index (NBI).

www.gro.gov.uk/gro/content General Registry Office. Certificate ordering service.

www.freebmd.org.uk FreeBMD. Database of birth, marriage and death indexes.

www.1911census.co.uk Information regarding the release of the 1911 census.

www.statistics.gov.uk/census2001/bicentenary/bicent2.html Census Area Monitors. Provides historical facts and comparisons over 200 year period.

www.historicaldirectories.org/hd Historical Directories.

www.nationalarchives.gov.uk/mdr The Manorial Documents Register at The National Archives.

www.windmillworld.com Lists mills across the region with some historical background.

www.breweryhistory.com Brewery History website. Includes lists of defunct breweries and descriptions of their liveries.

http://londonpublichouse.com Historical Directory of pubs in south east England.

www.slq.qld.gov.au/info/fh/convicts Lists convicts transported to Australia, 1787–1867.

www.memorialinscriptions.org.uk National Archive of Memorial Inscriptions (NAOMI). Growing database including nearly 600 Norfolk burial grounds and churches.

www.zetica.com Maps of unexploded ordnance across the region based on research in national and local archives.

www.charity-commission.gov.uk Charity Commission.

www.workhouses.org.uk Workhouses. Includes the history of most East Anglian workhouses with photographs.

www.homepages.rootsweb.ancestry.com/~spire/Yesterday/index.htm Examples from poor law records.

www.roll-of-honour.com Role of Honour. Lists war memorials with photographs and names.

www.ukniwm.org.uk The National Inventory of War Memorials. Growing database aiming to list every war memorial in the UK.

www.harry-tates.org.uk Harry Tate's Navy. Dedicated to the history of the Royal Naval Patrol Service. Includes video clips and memoirs.

www.thegenealogist.co.uk The Genealogist. Commercial website offering access to a wide range of indexes and records including nonconformist.

www.nationalarchives.gov.uk/hospitalrecords The National Archives and Wellcome Institute catalogue of records from over 1,000 hospitals.

www.auod93.dsl.pipex.com/Companies.htm Index to East Anglian railway companies with a summary of their history.

www.trap.org.uk/FamHist.html Tracking Railways Archives Project aims to list all railway archive collections.

www.transporttrust.com/10078.html Red Wheel. Celebrates Britain's transport legacy by marking sites of special historic interest with a Red Wheel plaque carrying links to a dedicated website.

www.scienceandsociety.co.uk Science and Society Picture Library. Includes selection of railway photographs.

Other Useful Organizations and Resources

Cambridgeshire

Cambridgeshire Family History Society
David Wratten, 43 Eachard Road, Cambridge CB3 0HZ
Email: secretary@cfhs.org.uk
www.cfhs.org.uk

Cambridgeshire and the Isle of Ely area

Cambridgeshire Record Society
c/o Cambridgeshire Archives
Box RES 1009. Shire Hall
Castle Hill, Cambridge CB3 0AP.
Tel: 01223 364706
Email: info@cambsrecordsociety.co.uk
www.cambsrecordsociety.co.uk

Fenland Family History Society
Membership: Anita Brown, Sunset Lodge, Station Road, Parson Drove,
Wisbech PE13 4HA
Email: secretary@fenlandfhs.org.uk
www.fenlandfhs.org.uk
Former Isle of Ely, part of south Lincolnshire and west Norfolk area.

Huntingdonshire Family History Society
c/o Membership Secretary, Mrs G Tompson, 1 Hoo Close, Buckden, St Neots
PE29 5TX
Email: bookstall@huntsfhs.org.co.uk
www.huntsfhs.org.uk

Essex

Essex Society for Archaeology and History
Membership: Miss Ann Turner, 1 Robin Close, Great Bentley, Colchester CO7
8QH
www.essex.ac.uk/history/esah

Essex Society for Family History
ESFH Research Centre, c/o Essex Record, Office, Wharf Road, Chelmsford CM2 6YT
Tel: 01245 244670
Email: office@esfh.org.uk
www.esfh.org.uk

Norfolk

Fenland Family History Society
Membership Secretary: Mrs Anita Brown, Sunset Lodge, Parson Drove, Wisbech PE13 4HA
www.fenlandfhs.org.uk

Mid Norfolk Family History Society
Membership: Joan Allson, 26 Recreation Road, Toftwood, Dereham NR19 1TB
Email: joanallson@hotmail.com
www.mnfhs.freeuk.com

Norfolk Family History Society
Kirby Hall, 70 St Giles Street, Norwich NR2 1LL
Tel: 01603 763718
Email: nfhs@paston.co.uk
www.norfolkfhs.org.uk

Norfolk Record Society
C/o 29 Cintra Road. Norwich NR1 4AE
Email: nrs@norfolkrecordssociety.org.uknospam
www.norfolkrecordsociety.org.uk

Suffolk

Suffolk Family History Society
Membership: Jean Licence, 60 Oldfield Road, Ipswich IP8 3SE
Email: membership@suffolkfhs.org.uk
www.suffolkfhs.co.uk

Suffolk Records Society
Hon Secretary, Claire Barker MA, Westhorpe Lodge, Westhorpe, Stowmarket
IP14 4TA
Tel: 01449 781078
Email: claire@ejbarker.co.uk
www.suffolkrecordssociety.com

General

Federation Of Family History Societies (Ffhs)
PO Box 8857, Lutterworth LE17 9BJ
Tel: 01455 203133
Email: admin@ffhs.org.uk
www.ffhs.org.uk
Contacts for family history societies across the country. Pay to View database.

Huguenot Family History Society
The Huguenot Library, The Huguenot Society, University College London,
Gower Street, London WC1E 6BT
Tel: 020 7679 7094
Email: secretary@huguenotsociety.org.uk
www.huguenotsociety.org.uk/family

Hyde Park Family History Centre
64–68 Exhibition Road, London SW7 2PA
020 7589 8561
Email: UK_LondonHydePark@LDSMail.net
www.hydeparkfhc.org

National Railway Museum in York
Leeman Road, York YO26 4XJ
Tel: 08704 214001
www.rm.org.uk
Includes library of railway publications and photographic collection dating
from the 1850s.

Railway Family Ancestors Family History Society
Mr J F Engert, Lundy, King Edward Street, Barmouth, Gwynedd LL42 1NY

Email: rafhs@btinternet.com
www.railwayancestors.org.uk
Wide ranging collection of sources and information on people associated
with the railway industry.

Museums, Heritage Centres and Places to Visit

Cambridgeshire

Bourne Mill
Caxton Road, Bourne
Reached via A1198 Royston to Huntingdon road. ¾ mile east of Caxton.
Contact: Janet Cornish, The Secretary, Cambridge Preservation Society.
Tel: 01223 243830
Email: thesec@cpswandlebury.org
Britain's oldest surviving post mill. Open various Sundays and by appointment.

Cambridge American Cemetery at Madingley
Madingley Road, Coton, Cambridge CB3 7PH
Tel: 01954 210350
www.gwydir.demon.co.uk/cambridgeuk/madcem.htm
Commemorates American service personnel killed or missing in action.

Farmland Museum & Denny Abbey
Ely Road, Waterbeach, Cambridge CB25 9PQ
Tel: 01223 860988
Email: info@farmlandmuseum.org.uk
www.dennyfarmlandmuseum.org.uk
Based in renovated farm buildings adjacent to Denny Abbey. The museum
the story of village life and Cambridgeshire farming.

Imperial War Museum, Duxford
Duxford CB22 4QR
Tel: 01223 835000
http://duxford.iwm.org.uk
Collection of over 150 historic aircraft and reconstructed wartime operations
room.

March and District Museum
High Street, March PE15 9JJ
Tel: 01354 655300
Email: info@marchmuseum.co.uk
www.marchmuseum.co.uk
Includes railway and military history, fenland drainage, a fenland cottage and working forge.

Museum of Technology, Cambridge
Old Pumping Station, Cheddards Lane, Cambridge CB5 8LD
Tel: 01223 368650
www.museumoftechnology.com
Housed in Victorian sewage pumping station and featuring local industrial technology.

Parson Drove Visitors Centre
The Village Green, Station Road, Parson Grove
Tel: 01945 700501
Email: thecage@parsondrove-pc.org.uk
www.parsondrove.com/cage.php
Interpretation and visitors centre housed in 'The Cage', a former jail, later housing the village fire pump. Displays include woad production.

Prickwillow Drainage Museum
Main Street, Prickwillow, Ely CB7 4UN
Tel: 01353 688360
Email: enquiries@prickwillow-engine-museum.co.uk
www.prickwillow-engine-museum.co.uk
Unique collection of large engines associated with the fens drainage housed in the original engine house.

Soham
Lodeside, Soham Village College, Soham
Plaque commemorating railway workers killed when ammunition train caught fire in 1944. Further details on this and the railway station can be found at: www.soham.org.uk/history/trainexplosion.htm

Stretham Old Engine near Wicken

From Cambridge head towards Ely on A10. Turn right at Stretham roundabout. Signposted road 400 metres on right.
Tel: 01353 648578
www.strethamoldengine.org.uk
Last of the ninety steam pumping engines installed throughout the Fens to replace 800 windmills. Open alternate Sundays April to September.

The Old Library, St John's College in Cambridge

St John's College, Cambridge CB2 1TP
Tel: 01223 339393
Email: jah63@cam.ac.uk
www.joh.cam.ac.uk/library/old_library
Internationally important collection of personal papers, manuscripts, books and photographs.

Whittlesey Museum

Town Hall, Market Street, Whittlesey, Peterborough PE7 1BD
Tel: 01733 840968
Displays include brickmaking, a blacksmith's forge and wheelwright's bench.

Essex

Ashdon Village Collection

Church Hill, Ashdon CB10 2HF
Tel: 01799 584253
Museum of Essex village life.

Bradford Street, Bocking

Sixty-five timber-framed buildings associated with the cloth trade, dating from at least the fifteenth to the nineteenth centuries.

Braintree District Museum

Town Hall Centre Gallery, Market Place, Braintree CM7 3YG
Tel: 01376 325266
Email: museum@braintree.gov.uk
www.enjoybraintree.co.uk/Museums-And-Culture/Braintree-District-Museum/Introduction.aspx

Exhibitions on local trades.

Braintree Silk Museum
Warners Mill, Silk Way, Braintree CM7 3GB
Tel: 01376 553393
Email: warner.archives@braintree.gov.uk
www.enjoybraintreedistrict.co.uk/Museums-And-Culture/Warner-Textile-Archive/Introduction.aspx
Housed in former silk mill. Includes the Warner Textile Archive.

Brightlingsea Museum
1 Duke Street, Brightlingsea, Colchester CO7 0EA
Tel: 01206 303384
Exhibits on the town's maritime connections and oyster industry.

Coggeshall Grange Barn
Grange Hill, Coggeshall, Colchester CO6 1RE
Tel: 01376 562226
Email: coggeshall@nationaltrust.org.uk
Thirteenth century timber-framed monastic barn.

Colchester Castle Museum
Castle Park, Colchester CO1 1TJ
Tel: 01206 282939
www.colchestermuseums.org.uk/castle/castle_index.html
Featuring many displays on Colchester's history from Roman times onwards, including the dungeons.

Colne Valley Railway
Castle Hedingham, Halstead, Essex. CO9 DZ. 01787 461174
www.colnevalleyrailway.co.uk
Steam locomotives, reconstructed station and miniature railway.

Dedham Vale
Essex village on the border of Suffolk in 'Constable Country'.
St Mary's Church in the village has wall shields depicting the Mayflower.

East Anglia Railway Museum
Chappel and Wakes Colne Station, Wakes Colne CO6 2DS
Tel: 01206 242525
www.earm.co.uk
Working museum dedicated to preserving railway history.

East Essex Aviation Society and Museum
Martello Tower, Point Clear, St Osyth, near Clacton-on-Sea CO16 8NG
Tel: 01255 434141
www.stosyth.gov.uk/default.asap?calltype=museum
Located in a Martello tower with local and US Air Force aviation, military
and naval displays.

Essex Police Museum
Contact: PO Box 2, Headquarters, Springfield, Chelmsford CM2 6DA
Tel: 01245 457150
Email: museum@essex.pnn.police.uk
www.essex.police.uk/museum

Great Dunmow Museum
Mill Lane, Dunmow CM6 1BG
Tel: 01371 878979
Email: info@greatdunmowmuseum.org.uk
www.greatdunmowmuseum.org.net
Based in rare small timber-framed maltings.

Great Wigborough Church
St Stephens, Church Lane, Great Wigborough CO5 7RL
Plaque commemorating the Zeppelin L33 crash in 1916.

Museum of Harlow
Muskham Road, Harlow CM20 2LF
Tel: 01279 454959
Email: tmoh@harlow.gov.uk
www.harlow.gov.uk/Default.aspx?page=7116
Includes displays on the town's history and original 'masterplan' for the new
town.

Paycoke's, Coggeshall
West Street, Coggeshall CO6 1NS
Tel: 01376 561305
Email: paycockes@nationaltrust.org.uk
www.nationaltrust.org.uk/main/w-paycockes
Late Gothic merchant's house, now a heritage centre housing displays of the renowned local lace and working wool loom.

Pound Green Close To Earls Colne
Village pump erected in 1853 by Mary Gee in thanks for the absence of cholera in the village.

Royal Gunpowder Mills, Waltham Abbey
Beaulieu Drive, Waltham Abbey EN9 1JY
Tel: 01992 707370
Email: info@royalgunpowdermills.com
www.royalgunpowdermills.com

Saffron Walden Museum
Museum Street, Saffron Walden CB10 1JL
Tel: 01799 510333
Email: museum@uttlesford.gov.uk
www.uttlesford.gov.uk/museum
Exhibits on the saffron and wool trades, timber framed buildings, public transport. A new Heritage Quest Centre will be built nearby in 2009.

Stansted Mountfitchet Windmill
Mill Hill, Stansted, Essex. SM24 8XX.
Tel: 01279 813124
Email: info@stanstedwindmill.co.uk
www.stanstedmountfitchetwindmill.co.uk/
One of the best preserved tower mills in the country.

Thorney Abbey St Mary And St Botolph Churchyard
Huguenot gravestones.

Thorrington Tide Mill
Three miles north-west of Brightlingsea, off the B1027. OS grid reference TM 0819. Only remaining tide mill in Essex. Open Bank holidays and the last Sunday every month.

Tower Windmill, Thaxted
Fishmarket Street, Thaxted, Great Dunmow CM6 2PG
Tel: 01371 830285
Rural life museum in a village famous for Morris dancing.

Townsford Mill
The Causeway, Halstead C09 1ET.
Tel: 01787 474451
Email: arnold.bradbury@ukgateway.net
Weatherboarded water mill built in the 1700s. Once part of the Courtauld textiles company. Now an antiques and heritage centre.

Tymperleys Clock Museum, Colchester
Trinity Street, Colchester CO1 1JN
Tel: 01206 282939
www.colchestermuseums.org.uk/tymperley/tymp_index.html

Upminster Windmill
St Mary's Lane, Upminster. RM14 2QH
Built in 1803 and retaining much of original equipment including grinding stones.

Norfolk

Bressingham Steam Museum
Bressingham near Diss IP22 2AB
Tel: 01379 686900
Email: info@bressingham.co.uk
www.bressingham.co.uk
One of world's finest collections of British and Continental locomotives, including the 'Royal Scot'.

Bridewell Museum

Bridewell Alley, Norwich, Norfolk NR2 1AQ
Tel: 01603 629127
Email: hannah.maddox@norfolk.gov.uk
www.museums.norfolk.gov.uk/default.asp?Document=200.22
Originally a prison for women and beggars. Now preserving the history of Norfolk's crafts and industries, including shoe making and a seventeenth century Jacquard loom.

Burston Strike School, Norfolk

Burston, Diss IP22 5TP
Tel: 01379 741565
www.burstonstrikeschool.org
Museum based in former school set up when local children went on strike in support of the village schoolteachers. Annual rally every April.

Carrow House Costume & Textile Study Centre, Norwich

301 King Street, Norwich NR1 2TN
Tel: 01603 223870
Email: museums@norfolk.gov.uk
www.museums.norfolk.gov.uk/default.asp?Document=210.10x1
Formerly the home of the Colman family, now housing a costume and textile collection dating from the eighteenth century. Open by appointment only.

Castle Rising Almshouses

East of the church, Castle Rising.

Colman's Mustard Shop

Royal Arcade, Norwich NR2 1NQ
Tel: 01603 627889
Email: avril.houseago@unilver.com
www.colmansmustardshop.com
Features displays of vintage containers and advertisements.

Coltishall Limekiln

Access via the adjacent Railway Tavern in Station Road. Access may be restricted between October and March due to hibernating bats.

Denver Sluice
Downham Market, Norfolk. On the River Great Ouse, 1 mile south of Downham Market. OS grid reference TF 5800
Originally built in 1651 by Vermuyden as part of the fens drainage scheme.

Dragon Hall, Norwich
115–123 King Street, Norwich NR1 1QE
Tel: 01603 663922
Email: dragon.hall@virgin.net
www.dragonhall.org
Rare medieval merchants trading hall built in the mid-fifteenth century.

Fakenham Museum of Gas and Local History
Hempton Road, Fakenham NR21 7LA
Tel: 01328 851696
Based in former gasworks.

Gressenhall Farm and Workhouse Museum of Norfolk Life
Gressenhall, Dereham NR20 4DT
Tel: 01362 860563
Email: gressenhall.museum@norfolk.gov.uk
www.museums.norfolk.gov.uk
Museum based in former workhouse complex and traditional farm. Displays and living history days on workhouse history and rural life.

Great Bircham Windmill
Great Bircham, Norfolk PE31 6SJ
Tel: 01485 578393
Email: info@birchamwindmill.co.uk
www.birchamwindmill.co.uk
Fully restored windmill and bakery. Open April to September.

Great Hospital, Norwich
Bishopgate, Norwich NR1 4EL
Tel: 01603 622022
www.thegreathospital.co.uk
Residential and sheltered accommodation dating back to the thirteenth century. Open days and tours by arrangement.

Great Massingham, Norfolk
Annual display of artefacts associated with the now disused airfield east of the village, which was a centre for Bomber Command. See Massingham Historical Society website for information: www.greatmassingham.net/page5.html

Great Yarmouth Rows
Remains of medieval network of courtyards and alleys in the centre of the town.

Henry Blogg Lifeboat Museum, Cromer
The Rocket House, The Gangway, Cromer NR27 9ET
Tel: 0123 511294
Tells the story of the lifeboat service and coxswain Henry Blogg.

How Hill Study Centre
How Hill Trust, Ludham, Norfolk NR29 5PG
Tel: 01692 678555
www.how-hill.org.uk
Environmental study centre. Includes Toad Hole Cottage Museum featuring Victorian life on the Broads.

Museum of The Broads
The Staithe, Stalham, Norfolk NR12 9DA
Tel: 01692 581681
Email: info@museumofthebroads.org.uk
www.northnorfolk.org/museumofthebroads
Waterside museum of broads life based in traditional buildings associated with the wherry trade.

North Norfolk Railway
Sheringham Station, Station Approach, Sheringham NR26 8RA
Email: enquiries@nnrailway.co.uk
www.nnrailway.co.uk

Norwich Castle Museum
Castle Meadow, Norwich NR1 3JU
Tel: 01603 493625

Email: museums@norfolk.gov.uk
www.museums.norfolk.gov.uk/default.asp?Document=200.21
Includes former dungeons with instruments of torture and death masks of some of prisoners executed here.

Norwich Cemetery
Earlham Road, Norwich NR2 3RG
Soldiers plot in the north-east corner.

Norwich Guildhall
Gaol Hill, Norwich NR2 1NF
Built in 1407–13, it now houses a tea room and displays of memorabilia relating to the Caley's chocolate works.
Also the home of the Norwich Heritage Economic and Regeneration Trust (HEART) www.heritagecity.org

Rosary Cemetery
Rosary Road, Thorpe, Norwich
Britain's oldest cemetery.

St George's Guildhall, Kings Lynn
29 King Street, King's Lynn PE30 1HA
Tel: 01553 765565
Email: stgeorgesguildhall@nationaltrust.org.uk
www.nationaltrust.org.uk/main/w-stgeorgesguildhall
England's oldest surviving guildhall. Now used as an art centre and theatre.

St James' Mill, Norwich
Whitefriars, Norwich NR3 1SH
Information: www.norwich12.co.uk/st-james-mill/who.htm
Grade One listed former steam-powered yarn mill dating from 1836. Occasional open days.

Sheringham Museum
Station Road, Sheringham (new museum due to open nearby in 2009).
www.sheringhammuseum.co.uk/index.html
Celebrates the town's lifeboat and fishing tradition.

Strangers Hall Museum, Norwich
Charing Cross, Norwich NR2 4AL
Tel: 01603 493625
Email: museums@norfolk.gov.uk
www.museums.norfolk.gov.uk/default.asp?document=200.23
Former merchant's house with many displays on trade in the area, including clothes and textiles.

Time and Tide Museum Great Yarmouth Life
Blackfriars Road, Great Yarmouth NR30 3BX
Tel: 01493 743930
Email: yarmouth.museums@norfolk.gov.uk
www.maritimeheritageeast.org.uk/museums/time-and-tide-museum-of-great-yarmouth-life
Features the town's fishing and maritime heritage.

Town House Museum of Lynn Life
46 Queen Street, King's Lynn PE30 5DQ
Tel: 01553 773450
Email: townhouse.museum@norfolk.gov.uk
www.maritimeheritageeast.org.uk/museums/town-house-museum

Wymondham Heritage Museum
The Bridewell Norwich Road, Wymondham NR18 ONS
Tel: 01953 600205
Email: info@wymondhamheritagemuseum.co.uk
www.wymondhamheritagemuseum.co.uk
Located in former prison, police station and court. Includes displays on local history, including crime and punishment and Kett's Rebellion.

Wymondham Railway Station
Station Approach, Station Road, Wymondham NR18 0JZ
Email: info@wymondham-station.com
www.wymondham-station.com
Restored working station housing a museum.

2nd Air Division Memorial Library, Norwich
The Forum, Millennium Plain, Norwich NR2 1AW
Tel: 01603 774747
Email: 2ndmemorial.lib@norfolk.gov.uk
www.2ndair.org.uk
2nd Air Division of the USAAF memorial library and roll of honour.

100th Bomb Group Memorial Museum
Common Road, Dickleburgh, Diss IP21 4PH
Tel: 01379 740708
Email: 100bgmm@tiscali.co.uk
www.aeroflight.co.uk/mus/uk/1-b/100thmus.htm
On the edge of the disused Dickleburgh airfield. Displays of USAAF decorations and uniforms, equipment, combat records and other memorabilia.

Suffolk

Alfred Corry Museum, Southwold
Ferry Road, Southwold IP18 6NG
Tel: 01502 723200
http://freespace.virgin.net/david.cragie/index.htm
Features the Alfred Corry lifeboat dedicated in 1893 and in service until 1918.

Armada Post, Lowestoft
Martin's Score, Lowestoft
Commemorative post to the Battle of the Armada in 1588.

Bawdsey Radar Museum
Bawdsey Quay, Bawdsey IP12 3AZ
Tel: 07821 162879
Email: info@bawdseyradargroup.co.uk
www.bawdseyradargroup.co.uk
Home of the first radar station in the world.

Brandon Heritage Centre
George Street, Brandon IP27 0PX
www.brandon-heritage.co.uk/heritage.html
Includes history of flint knapping and of warrenning in the area.

Clare
Once a centre for the wool trade in south Suffolk and renowned for the pargetting on many of its houses.

Framlingham Castle
Framlingham, Suffolk. IP13 9BP
Tel: 0870 3331181
www.english-heritage.org.uk/server/show/nav.12586
Twelfth century castle which became a prison and site of a parish poorhouse. Includes 'From Powerhouse to Poorhouse' exhibition exploring the history of people who lived in the castle since it was built.

Hadleigh Guildhall
The Guildhall, Hadleigh, Ipswich IP7 5DT
Contact: Jane Haylock 01473 827752
Dating from 1430 in what was once the third wealthiest town in Suffolk with many interesting buildings. Variable opening times. Group tours by arrangement.

Herringfleet Windpump
About 5 miles NW of Lowestoft, Suffolk. Access by footpath only from B1074 between St Olaves and Somerleyton.
Information: Mark Barnard, Suffolk County Council.
Tel: 01473 264755
Email: mark.barnard@et.suffolkcc.gov.uk
Broadland wind pump with cloth-spread sails and a boat-shaped cap.

Lavenham Guildhall
Market Place, Lavenham CO10 9QZ
Tel: 01787 247646
Email: lavenhamguildhall@nationaltrust.org.uk
Houses an exhibition on 700 years of the wool trade.

Little Hall, Lavenham
Market Place, Lavenham CO10 9QZ
Tel: 01787 248341
Email: info@littlehall.org.uk
www.littlehall.org.uk

Fifteenth century clothier's house, later divided into six homes. Now the home of the Suffolk Preservation Society and open to the public.

Lowestoft and East Suffolk Maritime Museum
Sparrows Nest Park, Whapload Road, Lowestoft NR32 1XG
Tel: 01502 561 963
Features model boats and fishing equipment in a flint built fisherman's cottage.

Lowestoft War Memorial Museum
Sparrow's Nest Gardens, Whapload Road, Lowestoft NR32 1XG
Dedicated to those who served during the Second World War.

Mid Suffolk Light Railway Museum
Wetheringsett
Email: chairman@mslr.org.uk
www.mslr.org.uk

Moyse's Hall Museum
Cornhill, Bury St Edmunds IP33 1DX
Tel: 01284 706183
Email: moyses.hall@stedsbc.gov.uk
www.moyseshall.org
Local and social history displays include a bust, death mask and account of the murder bound in the skin of the Red Barn' murderer William Corder.

Museum of East Anglian Life
Illiffe Way, Stowmarket, Suffolk IP14 1DL
Tel: 01449 612229
Email: enquiries@eastanglianlife.org.uk
www.eastanglianlife.org.uk
Includes displays and artefacts relating to rural life.

Offton Lime Kiln
Private land just north of the Limeburners public house. OS grid reference TM 0732 4935
Photographic display in the pub and on their website:
www.limeburners.co.uk/pub_history.htm

Orford, Suffolk
Traditional fishing village with many original buildings.

Otley Hall
Events Manager, Hall Lane, Otley, Suffolk IP6 9PA
Tel: 01473 890264
Email: enquiries@otleyhall.co.uk
www.otleyhall.co.uk/index_25.htm
Birthplace of Bartholomew Gosnold, explorer and pioneering American settler. Open days and private guided tours.

Pakenham Windmill And Watermill
Mill Road, Pakenham. Bury St Edmunds IP31 2NB
Windmill contact: 01359 230277
Watermill Tel: 01284 724075
www.pakenhamwatermill.co.uk
The only village in England to still have both a working windmill and watermill.

Parham Airfield Museum
Parham, Framlingham IP13 9AF
Tel: 01728 621373
Email: parhamairfield@yahoo.co.uk
www.parhamairfieldmuseum.co.uk
US 390th Bomb Group Memorial Air Museum and Museum of the British Resistance Organisation.

Royal Naval Patrol Museum
Sparrow's Nest Gardens, Whapload Road, Lowestoft NR32 1XG
Email: rnps_mus@lowestoft.org.uk
www.rnps.lowestoft.org.uk/index.htm
Commemorates the minesweeping service with displays including photographs, documents and uniforms.

Saxmundham Museum
49 High Street, Saxmundham
www.saxmundham.org/touristinfo/museum.html
Includes a 1930s scale model of the station as it was in the 1930s.

Saxtead Green Post Mill
Saxtead, Suffolk IP13 9QQ
One of the finest windmills remaining in England. Still in working order.

The Sailor's Reading Room Museum, Southwold
East Street, Southwold IP18 6EH
Dedicated to the history of Southwold, with a strong focus on fishing.

Wortham
Near Wortham church, Redgrave Road, Wortham
Memorial to the tithe wars of the 1930s.

Select Bibliography

Bailey, Mark, Jurkowski, Maureen & Rawcliffe, Carole, eds. *Poverty and Wealth. Sheep, Taxation and Charity in Late Medieval Norfolk*, Norfolk Record Society, Vol. LXXXI, 2007

Bennett, H S, *The Pastons And Their England*, Cambridge University Press, 1995

Bosworth, G F, *Essex*, Cambridge University Press, 1922

Burnay, Suzanna G, *Suffolk Snapshots*, (series) Sigma Books, 2000–2006

Blomefield, Francis, Parkin, Charles, ed.,*An essay towards a topographical history of the County of Norfolk*, William Miller, 1805

Brown, A F J, *Essex at Work, 1700–1815*, Essex Record Office, 1969

— *Prosperity And Poverty. Rural Essex, 1700–1815*, Essex Record Office, 1996

Cambridgeshire Family History Society, *Gamlingay: Portrait of an English Village*, Cambridgeshire Family History Society

Clark, Ross, *Cambridgeshire*, Pimlico County Guides, 1996

Coldham, Peter Wilson, *The Complete Book of Emigrants in Bondage, 1614–1775*, Baltimore: Genealogical Publishing Co Inc, 1988

Colman,Helen Caroline, *Jeremiah James Colman*, Chiswick Press, 1905

Cozens-Hardy, Basil & King, Ernest A, *The Mayors of Norwich 1403 to 1835*, Jarrold, 1938

Defoe, Daniel, *Tour Through Eastern Counties of England, 1722*, Project Gutenberg E-book at: www.bookrags.com/ebooks/983

Denson, John, *A Peasant's Voice to Landowners by John Denson of Waterbeach*, Cambridge Record Society, Vol. 9, 1991

Duncan, J, *The History of Presbyterians in Bury St Edmunds*, Journal of the Presbyterian Society Vol. 12, 1960–63

Edwards, A C, *A History of Essex*, Phillimore, 2000

Edwards, B, *The Burston School Strike*, Lawrence and Wishart, 1974

Edwards, George, *From Crow-scaring to Westminster*, np, London, 1922

Edwards, Peter, *Rural Life: Guide To Local Records*, B T Batsford Ltd, London, 1993

Feather, Fred, ed, *Tales From The Essex Police Museum*, Essex Family Historian Supplement, Dec 2007

Fletcher, Ronald, ed, *The Biography of A Victorian Village; Richard Cobbold's account of Wortham, Suffolk 1860*, B T Batsford, Ltd., 1977

Foster, M. Whitfield, *A Comedy of Errors or The Marriage Record of England & Wales 1837–1899*, np, Wellington, New Zealand, 1998

Fowler, Simon, *Tracing Your Army Ancestors*, Pen & Sword, 2006

— *Workhouses*, TNA, 2007

Frogley, Mr, *The Frogley Index and Manuscript*, EoLFHS CD, 2003

Gibson, J S and Medlycott, ##FIRST NAME?###*Militia Lists and Musters, 1757–1876*, 4th edn. FFHS, 2000

Gibson, J and Rogers, C, *Electoral Registers since 1832*, FFHS, 1989

Gibson, Jeremy, *Poor Law Unions*, Vols. 1–4, FFHS, 1997–2000

Grannum, Karen and Taylor, Nigel, *Wills and Other Probate Records*, TNA, 2004

Haining, Peter, *Maria Marten. The Murder in The Red Barn*, Images, 1992

Herber, Mark D, *Ancestral Trails*, Society of Genealogists, 2000

Hibbard, Henry, *A History of Burnham Thorpe. Lord Nelson's Birthplace,*. Revd C J Isaacson, The Burnhams Rectory, 1937

Hussey, Stephen, *Headline History*, Essex Record Office, 2000

Jebb, Miles, *Suffolk*, Pimlico County Guides, 1995

James, Zita ed, *Within Living Memory: A Collection of Norfolk Reminiscences*, Norfolk Federation of Women's Institutes, Boydell Press, 1972

Ketton-Cremer, R W, *A Norfolk Gallery*, Faber, 1948

Lloyd, David W, *The Making of English Towns. 2000 years of evolution*, Victor Gollanz Ltd., 1992

Mackie, Charles, *Norfolk Annals. Vols. I & II*, Norfolk, 1901

McCurrach, M, *Freemen of the Borough of Ipswich. Parts 1–2*, SFHS, 1997 & 2000

Meeres, Frank, *A History of Norwich*, Phillimore, 1998

Nissel, M, *People Count – A History of the General Register Office*, London, HMSO, 1987

Norwich, John Julius, *A Country Parson: James Woodforde's Diary 1759–1802*, Tiger Books International, 1991

Murphy, Michael, *Cambridgeshire and Opinion, 1780–1850*, Cambridge, 1977

Oppitz, Leslie, *East Anglia Railways Remembered*, Countryside Books, 1989

Pocock, Tom, *Norfolk* Pimlico County Guides, 1995

Norfolk Record Office,*Guide to Genealogical Sources*, 3rd edn. NRO, 1993

Norfolk Recorders, *Norfolk Allotments – the plot so far*, Norfolk Recorders, 2007 at: bondworks@phonecoop.coop

Rye, Walter,*Early life in the Manor of Burnham* in *Norfolk Antiquarian Miscellany*. *Vol. 1*, ed. Samuel Miller, Norwich, 1873
— *Norfolk Families*, Norwich, 1913
— *Pimlico County Histories. A History of Norfolk*, London, 1885
Stone, Michael, ed, *The Diary of John Longe, Vicar of Coddenham, 1765–1834*, Boydell Press, Suffolk Record Society, Vol. LI, 2008
Suffolk Family History Society. *Sudden Deaths in Suffolk and More Sudden Deaths in Suffolk*, SFHS CD, 2006
Tate, W E, *The Parish Chest*, 3rd edn. Phillimore, 1983
Tomaselli, Phil, *Tracing Your Air Force Ancestors*, Pen & Sword, 2007
Twinch, Carol, *The Little Book of Suffolk*, Breedon Books, 2007
Wenzenul, Rosemary, *Tracing Jewish Ancestors*, Pen & Sword, 2008
Whitehand, Ray, *At The Overseers Door*, Ray Whitehand www.historical suffolk.com / Publications_.html
Yorke, Trevor, *Tracing the History of Villages*, Countryside Books, 2001

Forthcoming Publications
Metters, Alan, ed, *A study of the King's Lynn Port Books 1610–1614*, Norfolk Record Society, 2009
Reeve, Keith, *Brothers in Methodism – Clement Reeve and the Cock Families of Northwold and Methwold in the mid-nineteenth Century*, author, Australia, 2009
Teasdale, Vivien, *Tracing Your Textile Ancestors*, Pen & Sword, 2009
Wilcox, Martin, *Fishing and Fishermen: A Guide for Family Historians*, Pen & Sword, 2009

Index